HOW TO KEEP LOVE ALIVE

Also by Ari Kiev, M.D.

Active Loving

The Courage to Live

Recovery from Depression

Riding Through the Downers, Hassles, Snags and Funks

A Strategy for Success

The Suicidal Patient: Recognition and Management

A Strategy for Handling Executive Stress

A Strategy for Daily Living

Transcultural Psychiatry

Curanderismo: Mexican-American Folk Psychiatry

Coping with Executive Stress (with Vera Kohn)

Mental Health in the Developing World: A Case Study in Latin
    America (with Mario Argandoña)

Edited by Ari Kiev, M.D.

Magic, Faith, and Healing: Studies in Primitive Psychiatry Today

Social Psychiatry: Eighteen Essays

How to Keep Love Alive

ARI KIEV, M.D.

BARNES & NOBLE BOOKS
A DIVISION OF HARPER & ROW, PUBLISHERS
New York, Cambridge, Philadelphia, San Francisco,
London, Mexico City, São Paulo, Sydney

A hardcover edition of this book is published by Harper & Row, Publishers, Inc.

First BARNES & NOBLE BOOKS edition published 1984.

Designer: Sidney Feinberg

Library of Congress Cataloging in Publication Data
Kiev, Ari
    How to keep love alive.
    1. Love.   2. Conflict (Psychology)   I. Title.
BF575.L8K494   1982   646.7′8   81-47661
ISBN 0-06-463596-1 (pbk.)   AACR2

84   85   86   87   88   10   9   8   7   6   5   4   3   2   1

For Phyllis

Contents

Introduction: Trusting the River

A college classmate of mine, Jack Campbell, recently told me of his latest annual canoe trip down one of the wild rivers of New England. Generally he goes alone, but this time he took along a business associate who had never been in "white water" before. While negotiating the rapids was tremendously exciting for my friend, his associate became quite nervous about capsizing, and in the end this nervousness almost killed both of them.

"We'd just come into the fast part," Jack told me later, "and the water had become pretty rough. Nothing we couldn't have handled, really, if Harry hadn't gone to pieces on me. Suddenly a big boulder appeared on the right and I yelled to him to lean left so the current could take us away from it. You know what he did instead?"

"Tried to push it away?"

"Worse than that," he said, shaking his head. "He leaned so far left we started to roll, and I guess he thought we were going over. So he stood up in the damn canoe and got ready to jump out! I couldn't believe it. We had a choice of scraping a boulder or capsizing—and he wanted to go over the side."

He smiled wryly as he recounted this close call, but you

could see it hadn't been very funny at the time.

" 'Sit the hell down!' I yelled at him, and that shocked him long enough so I could straighten us out. We rammed the rock all right, but not too bad. At least it dented the boat and not us. We still had a couple of hundred yards of the white to go, and I told him just to sit tight while I paddled. By that time, the situation had scared him too much for him to do anything else, so we made it out OK. I tell you, though, if I'd known he couldn't handle the risks calmly, I'd never have asked him along. It's hell on wheels going through rapids with somebody who doesn't trust the river."

Now, I don't know much about canoeing, but as I listened to Jack's story I realized that you don't have to be a wilderness buff to encounter "white water" in your life. Many years of working with people terrified and stymied by problems made me realize that this tale of near disaster could serve as an instructive parable for many of us who have never been near a wild river.

The story reinforced a lesson that had been demonstrated over and over again in my experience with patients: panicking in the face of trouble generally only aggravates the trouble, while keeping a cool head enables you to "ride out the rapids" of a situation, whether on a river or in your personal life.

Among my patients, those with the most productive and long-lived relationships have learned not only not to jump when the going got rough, but to "trust the river" enough to know that if they kept calm and rolled with the rapids, they would eventually ride through the danger. Conversely, those who were overwhelmed by their personal stretches of "white water" were those who saw the first sign of trouble as disaster.

In love, as in river running, success depends on trust—which means trusting *yourself*. Where people enter relationships, especially romantic ones, with an excess of dependency needs and expectations, where they do not trust themselves but practice what I have called "passive love" in my recent book *Active Loving*, you can expect that they will not be able to handle the inevitable conflicts of the relationship and that the relationship itself will be threatened.

In this book I want to consider how and why romantic conflict arises, giving special emphasis to the role of change in contemporary personal relationships. I am convinced that conflict and change *can* and *should* be productive to couples who sincerely want to turn their relationships around from a condition of intermittent bickering and decay to one of regeneration and growth, to relationships that are filled more with the positive rather than the destructive forces present in close involvements. This book focuses, therefore, on how to keep love fully alive—especially in the face of "white water," or conflict.

Most people tend to consider "trouble" in a relationship as a "bad thing" to be avoided at all costs. Like the novice canoer in the story, you may panic at the first sign of danger—and thus very often succeed in making matters worse. Since countless magazines, novels, and movies tell you that people who "really" love each other act in generous, open-minded, and tolerant ways, you may not know what to do with feelings of selfishness, resentment, and downright orneriness when they periodically occur. When you fight with your loved ones, you may think it is the beginning of the end. When your feelings or circumstances change faster than expected, you may think this presages doom. To forestall the anticipated breakup, you may jump up in the boat, start screaming and waving your arms at the rapids—and end up, all the sooner, in the drink.

Now, certainly no one believes today that relationships can exist without some conflict. The high divorce rate prevents us from deluding ourselves that true love lasts forever. Nevertheless, as the first chapter of this book shows, the image of love as life's crowning bliss that can make everything else all right still has a tenacious hold on the thinking of young people, both before and after marriage.

Many of these young people, persuaded by popular notions of the permanence of love, form relationships based on myth rather than reality, and when the going gets rough, as it invariably does in all human endeavors, they flee in bewilderment from the relationship, feeling both confused and betrayed. As dozens of my patients have pointed out, spouses rarely prove to be the shining knights or princesses that they thought they married. It takes considerable effort at times to help them to see that their *dreams*, not their partners, have betrayed them.

In this book I hope to point out the *inevitability of conflict and change in human relationships and how they can be used to help keep a troubled union alive*. While it may be easier to run from trouble than to face it, I hope to show that *the fear of trouble*, far more than the trouble itself, constitutes the real villain in personal misunderstanding. I'll try to point out, too, that the unwillingness to slow down, to talk things out, to negotiate solutions frequently spells the death of relationships even when the basic issues are minor. The terror of confronting unpleasant and potentially disruptive situations causes more interpersonal discord than the original situations themselves: jumping overboard, in other words, can be a lot worse than hitting a rock.

In this book, we will see first how the myth of romantic permanence has fostered unrealistic expectations about love that do not correspond to the realities of personal interactions. We will also see how the individual and collective rhythms that comprise interaction can, when understood and carefully managed, actually turn conflict into growth. We will discuss several common problems associated with interpersonal conflict, including communication impasses, dependency on the past, role playing, and the confusion of identity resulting from the "loss" of oneself in a relationship. Finally, we will consider ways you can successfully deal with change as well as how you can solve specific dilemmas, even when they seem to be apparently insoluble.

In personal relations, no less than in white water canoeing, trouble cannot be avoided. But the all-too-common methods of meeting that trouble—polarization, resentment, and silence—can be avoided. I hope this book will help you to learn How to Keep Love Alive and how to use change and conflict to your own and your partner's advantage. By learning to "trust the river" you can learn to cooperate better not only with your "partner in conflict" but also—and more importantly—with yourself. Once you have done that, you will be in a position to appreciate the truly exciting aspects of your relationship and will be able to move forward confidently into realms of uncertainty and excitement that until now you probably have avoided.

HOW TO KEEP LOVE ALIVE

Chapter 1

Happily Never After

On the surface George and Penny seemed like the perfect couple. High school sweethearts, they had married just after college, raised two bright and active youngsters, and established firm professional and personal contacts in their community. George's sales career had flourished, and Penny recently had taken a position as a buyer for a major department store. Things couldn't have looked smoother.

Beneath this pleasant social façade, however, the two lived in a state of turmoil. George appeared distracted, nervous, and bitter when he came to me for advice. Penny, he said, had stopped paying attention to him. "She's always at the damn store," he complained. "Her career means more to her than our marriage. I can't stand to see this happening to us."

They had been fighting, it turned out, almost from the day she had started work, and George evidently had been increasingly unable to tolerate her absence from the home, which he now sarcastically labeled their "little love nest."

"When I first married Penny, things ran smoothly. I'd come home from a day on the road and have dinner and read the kids a story and then we'd watch TV together until bedtime. Her job has changed all that. Why she wanted to take it in the first place I'll never know. We didn't need the money. I was perfectly able to support the family, and I liked doing it. It was the same way that my father and grandfather had supported their families. When we were back in high school . . . "

He trailed off, frowning over painful memories. "I just wish," he said emphatically, "that it could have been like that forever. I liked it the way we were."

The way we were. The phrase reverberated in my mind, and I thought of the dozens of times I had heard it or variations of it spoken with bitterness and pain by people such as George. For many years I had counseled couples whose principal source of friction was the discrepancy between their current situation and some ideal Golden Age of Love in their mutual past. George was not unique. In my experience, in fact, his anger at the way his marriage had changed over the years was a perfectly typical response.

I have treated many troubled couples whose vigorous and sometimes vicious conflicts over money or sex or the right way to raise their children invariably proved to be smoke screens for a more fundamental disappointment about the way their love had evolved into something neither of them had expected. In fact, they usually proved to be fighting over the fact that one or both of them now perceived their life as radically different from the way it had been perceived when they had first come together. Promises made had been broken. Things had not turned out as planned. They were no longer "the way they were."

What had caused the turmoil, in short, was *change*. No

matter how good or bad the present might be, it differed from the past, and for many couples this change disrupted their sense of security. In some cases the relationship actually dissolved over the partners' simple inability to adjust to the fact of change—since that change was construed as evidence that the relationship had gone downhill.

For many people in relationships, the governing idea seems to be that if things don't remain the same as they were in the "Good Old Days," then they're not worth preserving. They view change as a betrayal, a denial of the very grounds on which their relationship had been established. People who equate the notion of love with a well-defined, predictable home situation (such as that poignantly suggested by George's picture) tend to perceive change not as an opportunity for constructive alteration but as evidence of decay.

Love with a Capital L

Now, fear of change reflects the popular view of romantic love in Western society. In spite of modern skepticism and the high divorce rate, the fear of change continues to affect our thinking about relationships, whether they're firm marital unions or "experimental" bonds.

According to this view, "real" or "true" or "romantic" love involves such profound manifestations of affection as sweaty palms, palpitations, dizziness, obsessive thinking, and the certitude that this relationship will meet all your dreams. Anyone who has read a Barbara Cartland novel or seen an old Hollywood movie will recognize the attitude I mean. It involves a conviction, basically, that a real union must be founded on a type of emotional response that is (1) instantly recognizable ("When you fall in love, you'll know it"); (2) completely irresistible ("He swept me off my feet"; and (3) immutable throughout time ("They lived happily ever after"). That response, which countless modern people still take to heart, might be called "Love with a capital L."

This static, adolescent notion of love has suffered somewhat under the onslaught of high divorce rates, situation ethics, serial monogamy, and even the more realistic character portrayals in recent movies, but it has lost little of its standing as a basic formula for popular novels and songs. In fact, most Westerners today still look forward to forming lasting relationships (marital or otherwise) based on the expectation that romantic love will conquer all obstacles in the end, rather than on the equally traditional grounds of kinship, position, or dowry. They come together for the same reason that George and Penny came together: because they feel themselves to be "in love."

Some people do marry to consolidate business enterprises or family position, but we tend to think of such relationships as somewhat callous and cold-hearted. While we may comment cynically that only a fool marries simply for love, we conceive that marrying for anything else makes you a bit of a knave. What Margaret Mead said midway through this century rings true today: "All the poetry, the phraseology, the expectation of marriage that would last 'until death do us part' has survived long after most states have adopted laws permitting cheap and quick divorces."*

We tend to think of this state of affairs, this business of modeling our relationships on fairy tales, as something that has been around forever. So long has the notion of

*Margaret Mead, *Male and Female* (New York: Dell, 1969), p. 334.

true love as a prerequisite for a real relationship been popular that you might assume it to be both a universal and an ancient phenomenon. Since everything from perfume ads to marriage vows celebrates romantic love as obvious, irresistible, and unchanging, we may easily assume it to be a reflection of human nature. But as sociologist William Graham Sumner observed in his classic study of human customs, "The notion that a man's wife is the nearest person in the world to him is a relatively modern notion, and one which is restricted to a comparatively small part of the human race."*

When did the notion of romantic love first make its appearance? Well, in the West, where it enjoys the greatest popularity today, it has existed as a definable cultural sentiment for less than a thousand years. It may be hard to believe that something thought to be as deeply ingrained in humanity as romance has existed for such a short period of time, but in fact it was the poets of southern France at the end of the twelfth century who popularized the ecstasy so often praised in songs and Harlequin romances. The feeling of "being in love" is a widespread phenomenon and dates back at least as far as the Bible's *Song of Songs,* but our devotion to it as a social ideal has existed actually for only about eight hundred years.

The Origins of Romance

Sometime at the beginning of the thirteenth century, Eleanor of Aquitaine and her daughter, the Countess Marie of Champagne, summoned a French cleric named André le Chapelain (André the Chaplain) to the royal

*William Graham Sumner, *Folkways* (New York: Mentor, 1940), p. 312.

court at Poitiers to prepare a manual on courtly love. Poitiers at that time had become a haven for troubadors, and Marie had embarked on the project for which history would remember her: the creation of the West's first courtly society.

She needed, to further the scheme, a handbook of manners that would impart to her adventurers and soldiers the refinement they so conspicuously lacked. She wanted a manual "to draw men from the excitements of the tilt and the hunt, from dice and games to feminine society . . . to outlaw boorishness and compel the tribute of adulation to female majesty."* She turned to André for help.

The Chaplain's book, *De Arte Honeste Amandi* ("The Art of Courtly Love"), became one of the major cultural documents of its time. As a code of conduct for Marie's devoted retinue, it not only enabled courtesy to push martial spirit aside as a dominant public sentiment, it also established the major conventions for a kind of emotional experience—the experience of romantic love—that has remained an abiding social force up to the present day.

It would be difficult to exaggerate the influence that André's image of courtliness has had on our social behavior. Eight hundred years after he completed his task, the basic ideas of courtly love, though modified as we shall see, still affect the way men and women relate to each other. In her attempt to alter the rude manners of her entourage, Marie transformed forever some of the fundamental bases of relationships. In spite of the many sexual and social revolutions that have since occurred, the concept in the Western world of love, and ideas of how being

*Amy Kelly, *Eleanor of Aquitaine* (New York: Vintage, 1950), p. 208.

in love should feel, still derive in great measure from this dream born in twelfth-century France.

What did the dream entail? What ingredients in the courtly love tradition enabled it to survive for so long?

Historian Warren Hollister has described the importance of the Poitiers courtly tradition in the formation of our common view of love:

> It was from [the romantic-love tradition of] Southern France that Europe derived such concepts as the idealization of women, the importance of gallantry and courtesy, and the impulse to embroider relations between man and woman with potent emotional overtones of eternal oneness, undying devotion, agony and ecstasy.*

These notions clearly have meaning today. The essentially courtly ideas suggested here—to protect and revere women, to expect love to be both painful and joyful—still have profound influence among people today, even though we may think of the troubador tradition as effete and outmoded. The resistance to the Equal Rights Amendment, for example, may be seen on one level as a payment of allegiance to the medieval notion of love, which demands that women be kept on a pedestal and worshipped from afar. That notion, quaint as it may sound, has no dearth of modern champions.

The medieval ideal of courtly love has many complicated and subtle aspects that need not be analyzed in a book about a modern dilemma. But I do want to mention two of these aspects, because they illustrate in some measure the durability of the archaic ideal. While courtly love

*C. Warren Hollister, *Medieval Europe: A Short History* (New York: John Wiley, 1968), p. 239.

per se no longer exists, it still continues to influence present-day relationships in subtle ways, and its influence, ironically, makes it difficult for relationships to prosper.

One aspect of courtly love is that true love may be *incomplete*. This incomplete romance most often consisted of the distant adoration of a married woman. The man, hence, could never hope to consummate their union. While she might love him as strongly as he loved her, their love remained remote, unattainable, and unsatisfied. Love became an art or a science in this tradition (which the trouvères adhered to more strictly than the troubadors), but lost much of its humanity.

The customs of courtly love enabled a young man to express an essentially adulterous passion within the confines of a poetic convention. Moreover, the customs would keep veiled the sinful, and specifically, the Oedipal, implications of his desire. One should note that the courtly ideal and the cult of the Blessed Virgin appeared in France at about the same time. You can see why incompletion was tolerated, even encouraged. In the idealization of Mary, the mother of God, or Marie, the daughter of Aquitaine, the same sentiment existed: Nature often thwarted true love.

The idealization of the beloved, morever, stemmed from a *passion*, not a mutual affection. Here André's book expanded only a little on the Roman poet Ovid's notion of love as delicious pain. Passion, from the Latin, meant suffering, and the truly passionate lover would suffer terribly on his distant lady's account. As a contemporary put it, "Mortal love is but the licking of honey from thorns."* Or, in the more precise phrasing of a modern French

*Quoted in Kelly, *Eleanor of Aquitaine*, p. 211.

medievalist, "Passion is that form of love which refuses the immediate, avoids dealing with what is near, and if necessary invents distance in order to realize and exalt itself more completely."*

The critical dimension of *distance*, I should emphasize, did not emerge accidentally but evolved as a central element to the maintenance of the original romantic ideal. Incompleteness intensifies passion, while union reduces both passion and suffering and raises the spectre of adultery. The idea in the courtly conventions seemed to be to maintain a nonconsummated, quasi-adulterous attraction.

This kind of emotional framework could not mesh very well with the contrary social ideal of marriage. Conjugal union required partners to have offspring, and thus repeated sexual union, and to live lives of peace and harmony, thus violating the very foundation of courtly love. "Passion and marriage," says the historian of the Tristan myth, "are essentially irreconcilable. Their origins and their ends make them mutually exclusive."† In Marie's new polite society, true love ended, rather than began, with sex.

Another aspect of the courtly ideal, which continues to impact on contemporary mores, is the medieval notion of *constancy*. While not as popular a notion today, it played a major role in the medieval mind, because its aim was spiritual achievement. Society viewed the person with inconstant attitudes or desires as ignoble and false. The person who, amidst all the turns of fickle fortune, retained an unswerving dedication represented the best quality in

*Denis de Rougemont, *Love Declared* (Pantheon, 1963) p. 41
†Denis de Rougemont, *Love in the Western World* (New York: Harper Colophon, p. 277.

humanity, one that was an imitation of the immutability of the divine.

In terms of romantic love, though, this constancy was often attached to a remote and unresponsive ideal. The courtly lover who had chosen to devote himself to a lady was expected to continue his service though he might never be (physically) rewarded. He could maintain his constancy by convincing himself of the inestimable value of the *act* of loving itself, and of the rewards inherent in the suffering that attended it.

This gave the medieval lover a strange kind of freedom. Since he might expect that his affection would not be returned, he could practice "active loving": that is, he could love *without any expectation of return,* where the act of loving itself brings its own rewards and does not depend on reciprocation.

Romantic attachments that depend on mutual response lack the coherent self-containment of courtly love. The troubador who spent his time bemoaning his unrequited passion had at least the consolation of knowing the outcome in advance. His complaint, then, should be seen as a poetic conceit; since he could predict the outcome of his expressions of love, he did not have to contend with the critical ingredient of modern relationships, the fear of change.

Determined, unwavering constancy probably provides part of the reason for the attraction of the courtly ideal. Lovers who speak of their unions as being "gifts from God" or "marriages made in Heaven" reveal the religious origins of this notion of constancy. The idea of a union made immutable by God certainly appealed to the troubadors though, as we have seen, in a context where relationships were not always consummated in marriage.

Some six hundred years after André published his little book, the English poet John Keats suggested something of the nature of "obstructed constancy" in his famous "Ode on a Grecian Urn." The poet describes a scene of amorous frolicking painted on an urn. His description of one youth chasing another depicts the peculiar attractions of the original French ideal:

> Bold Lover, never, never canst thou kiss,
> Though winning near the goal—yet, do not grieve;
> She cannot fade, though thou hast not thy bliss,
> For ever wilt thou love, and she be fair!

Frozen in time, the lovers on the urn, in other words, cannot suffer any pangs of human inconstancy. The attraction of the courtly ideal, in Keats's day as in Marie's, must have been the assurance it gave the lover that his passion would never die, even if it was not returned. And, obstructed as it was, it could never come up against the devastating realization of the *constancy of change.*

Though the ideals of romantic love were exemplified more in the legends and writings of the times than in the lives of those who subscribed to the ideal, the influence of this convention continues to be prevalent, which the Georges of our world discover now—often too late—to their regret.

True Love Marches On

The Chaplain's myth of obstructed constancy did not fade away. Since his death its influence has extended to every branch of European art and culture. Denis de Rougemont, in fact, calls this myth of unrequited passion "the secret which Europe has never allowed to be given

away, a secret it has always repressed—and preserved."*
Some idea of its resilience in the consciousness of the West
may be gained by noting only a few of the many major
cultural achievements that, over the years, have relied on
it as a central motif:

- It possessed the Italian poet Dante, generally acknowledged to be the most influential writer of the late
middle ages. *The Divine Comedy* and many of his
other works owe their origin to his obsession with one
Beatrice Portinari, the "muse" for whom he nurtured
a fervent and unrequited passion throughout his life.
(Francesco Petrarch, another great fourteenth-cen-
tury Italian author, wrote more worldly poetry, yet his
passion for Laura was very much akin to that of
Dante's for Beatrice.)

- During the Elizabethan Renaissance of the late sixteenth and early seventeenth centuries, William
Shakespeare devoted his prodigious energies to several versions of the myth, including the poem *Venus
and Adonis* and the plays *Antony and Cleopatra* and
Romeo and Juliet. The latter, of course, stands as an
exemplary illustration of how interference with love
can actually excite its passion.

- In seventeenth-century France, the romance of unrequited love became a bookseller's principal standby.
The popular books of the now forgotten writers La
Calprenède and Mlle. de Scudéry were among "a long
series of works which preach a love of refinement and
a refinement of love; which inculcated a kind of sentimental playing at love, a subtlety of sighing for the

Ibid., p. 50.

unattainable loved one, with apparently no very genuine desire for her possession."*

- In 1774, the twenty-five-year-old Goethe's *Sorrows of Young Werther* galvanized all of Europe into romantic despair. The book gave tremendous impetus to the start of the Romantic Era—an era that lasted up to this century. It described in veiled terms the author's unhappy fascination with the fiancée of one of his friends.

- The operas of Richard Wagner achieved phenomenal success in the nineteenth-century musical world. The heroes of four of them—*Lohengrin, Tannhäuser, Tristan und Isolde,* and *Parsifal*—were medieval knights whose stories of unconsummated love and heroic devotion were treated at length in ancient legends.

- In our own century, the myth has continued to thrive, not only in the world of letters but in that predominantly sentimental genre, the cinema, as well. The two films, for example, that a recent poll found to be the most popular American movies of all time both use unrequited love as their central dramatic theme. The star-crossed affair of Scarlett O'Hara and Rhett Butler provides the main thread of *Gone With the Wind*, while the impossibility of union between "Mister Rick" and Ilsa is the governing motif of *Casablanca.* If the lesson needs repeating, we have only to recall the huge success, only a few years ago, of Erich Segal's poignant *Love Story:* like *Gone With the Wind*, it became one of the top money-making films of all time.

So we see that, in spite of the vastly different social milieux in which the authors lived, the theme of frustrated but constant passion has remained a central one in our

*W. H. Lewis, *The Splendid Century* (New York: Anchor, 1957), p. 265.

culture. People—whether in sixteenth-century England, eighteenth-century Germany, or the United States today —have always been eager to hear about constancy obstructed and the denial of True Love.

Having It Both Ways

The romantic literature of our day, however, has turned this tragic motif on end. For the first time in over eight hundred years, we find a nontragic view of romance to be overwhelmingly popular. This view, in its avid embrace of a kind of moonlight-and-roses optimism, satisfies the need for what I have elsewhere called "easy way" philosophies of living. These philosophies provide a form of instant gratification, but they are not in harmony with our more traditional awareness of the tragic nature of life and love.

I'm referring to a body of escapist and sentimental novels that you see hawked so frequently as "your ticket to exotic romance," and which millions of would-be lovers each year devour ravenously. The British novelist Barbara Cartland has become the acknowledged "queen" of this relatively new romance genre, while Ontario-based Harlequin Enterprises has become the industry leader in the production of its novels. Harlequin alone produces over two hundred titles each year, while the redoubtable Mrs. Cartland, now in her seventy-ninth year, has sold over 100 million volumes of moonlight and roses since she began writing in the 1930s.

Modern romance follows a predictable formula. The basic story line goes something like this. A young, virginal heroine finds herself in some exotic locale caught in a "web of deceit and intrigue" that revolves around a

brooding, mysterious male stranger. The "chemistry" between them impels her to try to tap the good she sees in
him. She falls into danger. He rescues her. He is ex-
onerated from the accusations of others by rescuing her
from danger. They fall into each other's arms and she
discovers he has loved her all along.

The closing pages of these books usually suggest that
the lovers' union, so long hindered by misunderstanding,
will now flourish more passionately than either could have
imagined, and that this passion will last, unchanging,
forever. The Cartland-Harlequin writers substitute a new
and benign myth of constancy in place of the myth of
obstructed constancy that had been the basis of European
romance for centuries. Whereas traditional romance de-
pended on the separation between passion and union,
modern romance washes it away in the soft-focus promise
that once the two lovers have wed they will remain in
exactly the same state of mind until the stars turn cold.

Today's romances, in other words, manage to have it
both ways. They propose that True Love can have both
the passion that comes from uncertainty and the peace of
mind that comes from a sense of a permanent and unchanging union. Romantic and conjugal love thus support
each other, as parts of a philosophy of immutable bliss that
might be called the philosophy of "reconstructed constancy." According to its axioms, all trouble, all conflict, all
change cease once the lovers enter that last-page embrace. The close of Mrs. Cartland's 1974 novel *The Dangerous Dandy* is a good example of the tone of the school:
"Then as he drew her closer and closer still, he swept her
away into a Heaven where they were part of the Divine,
no longer two people but one, through all eternity."

Note the number of sentimental clichés that uplifting

coda contains. Consider first of all the notion that love "takes you over," or "sweeps you away"—that it's a phenomenon beyond your conscious control. Consider also the notion that its power comes somewhere from above —and because it's divinely inspired its claims should not be denied. Note also the assumption that love dissolves the differences between people, and that once you've found it, you will never again be without it.

Most important, however, is the idea that a mutual merging of souls, a willingness to give in to the "divine," can solve any problems, forever. This assumption has the appeal of a quick-fix medicine. Yet, paradoxically, the conviction that "love conquers all" has probably caused, directly or indirectly, more breakups than alcoholism, sexual maladjustment, or money problems.

Amor Vincit What?

As George and Penny could tell you, and as nearly one-half the couples married less than two years could tell you, love simply does not conquer all. The view of love as an unchanging, conflict-free passion makes sense only as a device of booksellers and songwriters, not as a reflection of reality. In fact, there may actually be an *inverse* relationship between belief in this kind of True Love and success in actual romantic unions. Almost certainly there is a connection between today's extremely high divorce rate and the unrealistic expectations that people bring to relationships.

I am not suggesting that paperback novels have caused the current astronomical breakup rate. I am merely citing these as elements in a general atmosphere inimical to lasting relationships—an atmosphere that applauds the ecstatic side of passion, but denigrates or ignores the suffering, patient side. Since the religious and social institutions that kept shaky marriages together in the past no longer have the same effect, many young people find it easier to abandon a less than satisfying union at the first opportunity rather than to work—and suffer—for its improvement. It may be the courts, and our own impatience, that end so many unions so quickly; but the myth of "reconstructed constancy" has done a good deal to point out to us where those unions have fallen short of the mark. "Where a couple have married in obedience to a romance," said de Rougemont, "it is natural that the first time a conflict of temperament or of taste becomes manifest the parties should each ask themselves: 'Why did I marry?' "*

We may marry because of a passion, but we expect the passion to outlast the honeymoon. This explains why modern lovers experience so much more bitter, and conflict-enhancing, disillusionment, than their medieval counterparts. A high breakup rate seems a natural result of the merger of passion and union demanded by the modern romantic myth. In de Rougemont's satirical phrasing, "To try to base marriage on a form of love which is unstable by definition is really to benefit the State of Nevada."†

The "variable," "unpredictable," "unstable," or "changing" character of romantic love gives it both its peculiar excitement and its terrible fragility. To make long-term relationships more than a series of fitful passions, we must come to terms with the changing or unpre-

*De Rougement, *Love in the Western World*, p. 292.
†*Ibid.*

dictable aspect of romantic love. By contrast, to follow the romantic novelists' approach to love, and disregard this dimension, leads not to bliss, but to bust.

Keeping your love alive, in other words, does not come as a stable, stainless-forever gift, divine or otherwise. Keeping love alive requires hard work; and to work at it effectively you must first recognize that constancy—whether obstructed or reconstructed—cannot be counted on as a day-to-day element of human union.

Setting your sights on keeping things "the way they were," therefore, leads only to disappointment. Only in movies and novels do things always remain the same. Relying on the divinely painful ecstasy of traditional romance, or on the divinely painless swoon of modern romance, will always cause problems. For sooner or later, even the most misty-eyed gazing of two lovers will pass as they discover that their "undying love" has changed.

I don't mean to imply by this that all relationships will fail. On the contrary, we all know of unions that last a very long time. The unions that have the best chances of success over time, however, view conflict and change as inevitable, and even as opportunities for growth, rather than as signs of decline. The people in those relationships, by and large, learn how to deal with each other not in books or movies or songs but in the hard, day-to-day crucible of living. They learn not to fear, but to manage, the inevitability of change.

Because the survival of love depends on the management of change, we will move next to a discussion of different types of change, and to how they impinge on certain areas of human conflict and growth.

Chapter 2

How Relationships Fail

The Christian religion, the dominant religious tradition in the Western world, for many centuries held marital unions together. Within the religious context people tolerated the natural vicissitudes of interpersonal life simply because those vicissitudes counted for less than the overriding concern of the Faith. It was not that couples from the twelfth to the nineteenth centuries didn't experience personal problems. They had the whole gamut of problems men and women have today, but their unions survived because divorce was virtually impossible. People were told that what God had joined together man was not allowed to sever. Besides annulment, the only other way out of a marriage was to separate—thus risking social disgrace.

Life without divorce—as you can easily imagine—was quite difficult. This explains why many of the revolutions against the Church proposed new laws on marriage and divorce. When Pope Clement VII refused to grant England's King Henry VIII an annulment, Henry broke with the Church—both personally and for all England—and set up Anglicanism (also known as the Church of England, or in America as Episcopalianism). By rejecting the dogma of marriage as a sacrament Anglicanism made marriage and divorce more of a civil matter. Martin Luther's revolution, which also took place in the sixteenth century, had the same effect.

With the increased availability of divorce, it shouldn't be surprising to discover the ties that bound marriages together became looser. In the modern secular world, which values personal choice and experience, it is possible to see the breaking of marriage vows as an act of virtue, given certain circumstances. In the absence of widely accepted religious strictures governing marriage, the termination of an unstable relationship does not present a major problem: one simply redraws the civil contract, acknowledging that things haven't worked out the way they were supposed to.

This means, paradoxically, that religious marriages may be more realistic about the future of a relationship than nonreligious ones. The couple who vow fidelity to an unchanging law have a better chance of fulfilling it than the couple who have come together on the simple understanding that they cannot bear to live apart. As soon as the natural rhythm of human interaction sets in, such a union often becomes prone to shifts of feeling and mood.

The modern myth of eternal romance thus makes it easy for people to forget the inevitability of ups and downs. Indeed, as we have seen, romance fiction throws a quasi-religious aura around the notion of falling in love, and denies the existence of change or conflict.

The poets' notions of constancy, eternal fidelity, and starry-eyed affection have themselves contributed to the breakup of many unions, simply because they have given people false ideas of what to expect from each other and from the union itself. No one but a visionary would consider the last half of the twentieth century a particularly good era for deep and lasting relationships. But this shouldn't be cause for despair. Understanding why so many relationships fail today is an excellent start toward learning how to avoid becoming one more divorce statistic. To that end, this chapter outlines what the alert person can expect on that tricky and exciting journey into mutual affection. Granted, my view of love may not be as pleasant or heart-fluttering as Wagner's or Barbara Cartland's, but it will be more realistic.

Problem One: History

The romantic conventions suggest that love happens to people outside of the constraints of space and time. On a given day in May, bells ring, time stops, and life begins over again from the moment the two lucky souls first look into each other's eyes.

The concept of "love at first sight," idyllic though it may be, does not hold up to close scrutiny. Although you may feel an intense attraction to someone the first time you see him or her, it will not be the first time you have ever looked at someone or listened to a sweet voice or an ingenious way of phrasing things. As unique and timeless as a relationship may seem to be, in actual fact you bring to it—to those eyes and that voice and that way of speaking—a huge array of understandings and expectations based on things that have happened before the two of you ever met. In other words, you bring your own *history* to the interchange. baggage??

Nobody comes to a relationship pure, without past experiences. We all drag along perspectives and attitudes conditioned by the past, and these perspectives necessarily color the way we relate to the other person. They include the false romantic expectations discussed in the previous chapter, as well as such unavoidable and seemingly innocuous elements of past history as the following:

1. *Family history*. The Biblical injunction advises a person about to be married to "forsake" his or her father and mother and "cleave" to the spouse-to-be (Gen. 2:24). Unfortunately, that is virtually impossible to do, as each person carries aspects of his parents within him. Young married people frequently fail to recognize that the person they marry has elements of his parents in him, as well as many expectations built up in childhood about what marriage should be like. Johnny may think he's free of his folks when he asks Sue to marry him, but after the wedding Sue (and he) soon discovers that he has a lot of his father in him —and this may be something she had not bargained for. Moreover, she also brings expectations to the union. Perhaps her father treated her mother like a queen—a behavior pattern she now expects from her husband. Unless Johnny has grown up in the same kind of family environment, his inability to reproduce certain aspects of her cherished childhood experience will lead to difficulties when they start living together.

2. *Birth order*. An enormous number of difficulties stem from early family situations, the most significant being the tensions inherent in the differing ways that parents treat older and younger siblings—and the way they treat each other. The birth-order factor can be a particularly complicated (and complicating) individual problem within the general arena of family history.

Say Johnny has two younger sisters who usually helped their mother around the house by waiting on the "men," Dad and Johnny. Johnny may be unaware of the built-in expectations derived from this early experience until he and Sue move in together. If she has been raised as an only child accustomed to making demands of others but not accustomed to being told what to do, he'll be taken aback when he complains that she has not darned his socks yet and she snaps back, "Darn them yourself!" Most of the interactional patterns people follow have been developed early in life, in relation to parents and siblings, and if two people with radically different patterns attempt to forge a life together, they can expect problems no matter how deep their love.

3. *Behavior patterns.* This holds true not only for patterns that evolve from sibling rivalry, but also for more general ways of relating to the world and to others. Suppose, for example, you came from a family in which emotion was suspect and in which family members customarily hid their feelings for fear of "offending" each other. If you bring this pattern of behavior with you to a marriage, you will run into difficulty the first time you disagree with your spouse and he or she asks you "What's wrong?" Modes of living that work within one family structure, in other words, can be disastrous when transported to a new context.

4. *Personality.* Personality factors also can provide real stumbling blocks to the progress of romantic attachment. In the heat of an initial infatuation, when sexual desire and wish-fulfillment take the place of conversation, personality easily can be overlooked. Yet personality—a combination of temperament, manner, and general outlook—can be more important than either sexual or intellectual affinity in the success of a relationship. Too few courting couples really take the time to assess their partners' personalities before marriage; as a result, they discover too

late that they have very little in common in terms of basic outlook or sensibility.

Personality presents relatively few problems in relationships in which "ecstasy" or "soul" or some other romantic intangible constitutes the hallmark of love. It had little significance, for example, for Romeo and Juliet. But had those two star-crossed lovers been given an opportunity to fulfill their single destiny in peace, they would have discovered that love consists of more than balconies and moonlight. Romeo might have discovered that Juliet took things too seriously for him; she might have found that she couldn't abide his constant singing.

Problem Two: Conflict Management

The sources of difficulty just mentioned—family history, birth order, behavior patterns, and personality—appear among virtually all human beings. In traditional societies various institutions were designed to help maintain the stability of marriage in spite of differing individual histories. But in a society such as ours, in which the traditional religious and social patterns of cohesion have all but broken down, individual differences become all the more important; without traditional stabilizers, the individual disagreements can easily lead to disaster.

Personal history, in other words, becomes much more important to consider in a society in which social history —the history of families within a community—has ceased to be a binding force. That is why it is crucial for couples today to weigh seriously the above elements before they commit themselves to a relationship. Failure to do so often leads to premature breakups and misery.

The problems of individual personal histories cannot be

overlooked. Since even identical twins have different past experiences, it must be that two people raised in different families, different towns, often different areas of the country, will clash over different interests and expectations that they bring to the marital situation. Reason dictates that two married people *must* confront the differences in their personal histories; if they perceive no such differences, they are still under a romantic spell, obliterating the lines between "mine," "yours," and "ours."

The problems of personal histories are twofold. First, people do not consider the past history, personality, and temperament of their potential partners; second, they know nothing about their own pasts either. Going along with the romantic illusion that they can "start anew" from the moment they meet, they assume that their own individual histories will have no real bearing on the outcome of a new relationship; that whatever differences in temperament or expectations exist, "true love" will right the balance.

In practice this means that most people investigate their own past history no more vigorously (and in some cases far less vigorously) than they do that of their partners-in-romance. As a result they buy not one, but two "pigs in a poke": the beloved (about whom they know little) and themselves (about whom they know only a little more). The result of this lack of concern for what makes up the characters in the union can be seen every day in the divorce courts. When a marriage starts out with two people refusing to consider their pasts, it's inevitable that conflict will arise.

Now, this would not be a tragedy if human beings had by this point in history, either personally or collectively, learned to *manage conflict* successfully. Unfortunately, the opposite holds true. The culture that links romantic love with an image of eternal bliss also accepts denial and avoidance of responsibility when dissension arises between lovers.

Few people learn to consider the real significance of relationships—i.e., the short-term and long-term significance. Few people learn usable methods of harnessing the reasons and purposes and tasks of their relationship, of managing their aggressive and disputational energies, so that when they come to the fore in romantic relationships (as they inevitably will), they face them largely mystified. Angry and afraid of their own turbulent emotions, they too often choose to suspend communication rather than seek help or try to work things out. And so the tragedy begins.

Problem Three: Growth

The tragedy develops as two people find that evolution, or growth, becomes threatening to one or both of them. I have seen this occur frequently among young married couples, like George and Penny, who entered marriage expecting things always to be The Way They Are Now. They forgot the absolute inevitability of change.

To manage conflict and change, you must learn to *incorporate* them into your relationship rather than try to escape from them. Differences can enrich a relationship and need not be a signal to separate. Unfortunately, too often young couples try to deny their differences and conflict, and as a result have great difficulty in handling trouble when it comes.

Various kinds of change occur in relationships, from the *individual* changes resulting from the unique growth process and life experience of each person; to *collective* changes that the couple experience as a unit; to *relational* changes reflecting the fluctuations and evolutions in the relationship itself. Each kind has its own pressures, anxieties, and joys. To use these changes to nourish rather than destroy your love, you must be able to anticipate and recognize them when they occur and know how to ride out their more difficult dimensions.

Growth can be painful and difficult, yet without it few relationships survive very long or very satisfactorily. Partners who, like Peter Pan, determine "never to grow up" usually find themselves, sometime later in their lives, unhappily married to children. This outcome, thankfully, can be prevented, but it takes conscious choice, and thoughtful action.

Sometimes, of course, growth means growth *away* from someone you once loved intensely. This can be painful. Occasionally growth makes separation or even divorce advisable. Often, however, when someone separates from a spouse to explore new aspects of himself or herself, he or she may re-create the same behavior patterns in the new relationship, thus beginning the whole cycle over again.

Patterns and Partners

Not too long ago, a patient of mine left his wife of twenty-five years for a much younger woman with whom he had fallen in love. His marriage had become "stale, predictable, and conflict-ridden," and the young woman held out to him the promise of freshness and newness. Things went well for about a year. Then he came to see me, depressed. "I'm feeling the same way about Margie now that I used to feel about Jane," he said glumly.

From a review of his story, it appeared that although the external circumstances of his life had altered, his own internal ways of dealing with things had not. He had brought to his second marriage precisely the same expectations and troublesome behavior patterns that had brought about the rupture of the first. Retrospectively he realized that he had failed to examine what troubled him and how he had created some of the problems that led to the breakup of his marriage. Lacking the knowledge that might have been gained from such an analysis, he merely recapitulated the past again in his new relationship, just as he had done in the first.

He had changed *partners* but not *patterns*. He had failed to develop new patterns of relating because he had not developed the interpersonal skills necessary for building satisfactory relationships.

These skills help couples to communicate without bitterness, to grow and not stagnate, to be free and not imprisoned. In fact they make it possible to sustain a loving relationship in the face of all the vicissitudes that a couple may face.

While each relationship has unique features to it, certain interactional patterns recur with sufficient regularity in all relationships to make it possible to rely upon general guidelines to assess the quality of the interaction. For this reason you can pick out certain patterns in successful love relationships, and spot the lack of these same patterns in unsuccessful ones.

Most people have the capability of improving and developing the basic ingredients of what may be considered the *capacity* to love. The critical step is to define these ingredients and learn to nourish them in order to increase the chances of keeping a loving relationship alive. The five most important elements of a loving relationship are as follows:

1. *The capacity to balance individuality (autonomy) and togetherness (mutuality)*
2. *The capacity to change over time*
3. *The capacity to escape the past*
4. *The capacity to express feelings*
5. *The capacity to listen*

Let's look at each of these a little more closely.

1. Balancing Autonomy and Mutuality

Human beings have a natural need for togetherness, for warmth and contact and mutual experience. In fact, when people have been denied these things early in life they have a good chance of developing antisocial or pathological behavior. Thus, the importance of close, loving relationships amounts almost to a biological need that contributes to making us complete and healthy human beings.

Human beings also have a not as easily recognized need for separateness. Ironically, it often seems easier to say yes to the group than to the single soul. Very often in relationships people deny their own need for individuality in order to give precedence to something that seems "bigger than both of us." This may lead to conflicts and resentment, especially when one feels an obligation to participate in this larger union rather than to interact in a freer fashion.

Loving couples need both *mutuality* and *autonomy*. One without the other cannot work, since an excess of autonomy leads to misunderstanding and separation. As a couple you must learn how to balance the demands of your individual needs for independence with the needs of the union. Only by doing this can you achieve a reasonable sense of togetherness without sacrificing the unique individual traits and needs that probably attracted you to each other in the first place.

In effect, most healthy relationships experience a kind of constant *push-pull,* as the needs of the individuals seesaw back and forth with those of the union. This can create a stimulating relationship, or it can cause worry and dissension. Couples who accept the fact that each person has needs that transcend the union will generally manage the push-pull well, while those who allow the union to take over their lives will end up disappointed and frustrated. It's a constantly shifting game of "Red Light," which can be won only with the proper balance of tact, concern, and patience.

2. Changing Over Time

Loving couples experience the push-pull of mutuality and autonomy every day of their lives together. The movement to and from the other that characterizes it is a given of daily interaction. Another aspect of the push-pull, however, takes place over a longer time span and must be carefully managed to avoid the twin dilemmas of isolation and severe dependency.

Relationships commonly go through long-range cycles of mutuality and autonomy, and understanding these cycles can help you anticipate and handle change productively. Generally the pattern looks something like this: The relationship begins with a phase of *approach,* in which the partners get to know each other. Next comes a *unity* phase, in which the needs of mutuality and common affection seem paramount. Finally comes a *separation* phase, in which individual needs come to the fore until the partners feel themselves to be too distinct from each other—which starts the approach phase, and the whole cycle, over again.

These phases may take a lifetime, but more commonly they recur in several-year periods, as the circumstances of the loving couple change and as they encounter experiences in their individual lives that require more or less closeness to their spouses. All couples undergo these changes at some time or another, however; so being aware of the inevitability of the approach-intimacy-separation cycle gives you a head start in being able to deal with its attendant problems.

Coping with long-term growth patterns, or life stages, constitutes a major aspect of this problem. Many couples enter their romantic unions resolved, like George and Penny, to stay serenely the same for fifty years, and it just doesn't happen like that. Handling change well means handling each other differently at fifty from the way you handled each other at twenty. People, after all, change over time and just as it would be unrealistic to expect that the adolescent's methods of interaction would be perfectly suited to his or her grandparents, so it is naïve to expect married partners to treat each other the same throughout the course of their union.

The person at fifty can and must be distinguished from the person at twenty. To cope with changes in attitude, expectations, behavior, and the like you must be sensitive to the *internal* and *external* variables that create changes in your life all the time. Unless you pay attention to these changes you will have difficulty in crossing new bridges, because you will have mistakenly assumed that the new bridges will be like the old.

3. Escaping the Past

Another necessary aspect of managing your stages of growth and change consists of learning to escape the constricting habits of the past—something that few people ever learn to do successfully. Family history, early behavior patterns, and birth-order roles all play a critical role in your development. These aspects of development can, if properly handled, be a means for self-understanding and greater fulfillment of personal capacities, but, unfortunately, for most people they serve not to liberate but to enchain. The patterns of interaction learned in childhood provide a kind of matrix against which all future development takes place. The tragedy is that most people take this matrix as an inflexible blueprint, not as a guide they can modify.

For example, people who grow up with extremely indulgent parents expect their future life partners to be just as indulgent, while people who have been constantly criticized may seek out partners who satisfy this need for criticism. In either case, they cannot easily shift out of an unpleasant pattern of living and prefer instead to stick with the known and familiar, no matter how painful or frustrating.

This pattern of compulsively repeating the past is disastrously common. Utilitarians would like us to believe that people in general act in their own best interests, but a first-year psychology student can tell you that this isn't the case. I have seen countless patients who have driven themselves to distraction by repeating their past patterns even when they are sources of extreme distress.

This type of repetition compulsion keeps people locked into familiar but unpleasant behavior. In dealing with a spouse, most people play specified *roles,* following *scripts* established as a result of the repetitive patterns and attitudes they bring to the relationship and the fixed interactional patterns that form early in the relationship. As a result of this they communicate and relate in predictably limited ways, rather than genuinely responding to the here and now of their mutual experience.

Escaping the past means becoming aware of the repetitive aspects of your behavior and by so doing being able to choose or control whether or not you will act in a nonrepetitive way in future situations. Despite powerful and pervasive influences, past patterns *can* be modified. Later on, I shall try to illustrate ways to utilize your own past experiences rather than be utilized by them, and show you how to rewrite the scripts that now govern your relationship.

4. Expressing Feelings

Before you can begin to change your counterproductive behavior, it's important to be able to see just what that behavior is about—from the inside as well as the outside. This is a sticky point for many people in close relationships. They can see that things aren't going well, but they don't really know how that is making them *feel,* and because they don't they often begin to express their dissatisfaction in an accusatory or hostile way, triggering defensive responses in their partners.

Before you can begin to turn a nonproductive relationship around, you have to be able to see how it is nonproductive. You have to see how aspects of it make you feel, and understand when your relationship is most vulnerable.

For example, in a marital therapy session I held recently with a young executive and his wife, the young woman repeatedly asserted that her husband made her "sick." "What do you mean by 'sick'?" I asked her. Only after much prodding did she describe the feeling as a sense of "emptiness in the stomach, and a growling, twisting hunger like pain." I turned to her husband and asked him if he had interpreted her use of the word "sick" in terms of this specific physical sensation. "No," he answered. "I always felt she was attacking me." "Would you have withdrawn from her if you had known she was referring to an actual physical discomfort?" I asked. "No. I would have tried to do something about it."

On the basis of his spontaneous responses, I persuaded her that telling him precisely how she felt might elicit understanding, while attacking him with accusations and complaints that he did not really understand only made matters worse. From this interchange they began to see how they each contributed to a communication gap that rapidly escalated into an emotional gap; they saw that by working together to explore and describe only their own feelings and not the explanations or causes of such feelings, they could improve the quality of their relationship.

"Getting in touch with your feelings" has been used too frequently and incorrectly to mean "letting off steam" rather than to describe the sensations associated with feelings. In fact, "feelings," especially the physical sensations involved, can be described in great detail and can help people to get to know one another better. Moreover, describing your feelings helps to *ground* discussions, giving them a specific focus, as well as allowing you and your partner to express your hurt and anxieties without vindictiveness and rancor. When hurt and anxiety are expressed in a calm, noncombative manner, it often brings surprisingly supportive responses from others.

5. Listening

Good relationships ultimately depend on good communication. Learning to be open about your feelings constitutes one major aspect of communication. A second important aspect is learning to listen to the other person without rancor or defensiveness.

Real listening of this type rarely occurs in romantic relationships. Few unhappily married couples faced with difficult decisions or strong differences really listen to each other. Instead, each party states his or her opinion, closes off the lines of reception until the other person has finished stating an opposite opinion, and then resumes the "discussion" by reiterating the same grievance again. Marital disagreements so often follow the same patterns over and over because the warring partners fail to recognize the unwritten rules, the nonverbal communication, and the attitudinal messages involved. Often it's these unwritten, unstated messages that keep them locked into repetitive scenarios, independent of the issues being considered.

Western culture encourages us to be *adversaries* in conversation. From childhood on we learn to debate, to use various gimmicks (satire, wit, marshaling of data) to overwhelm "opponents." We learn that winning is everything. We don't, however, learn basic principles of conflict resolution or decision making and so resort to argument when we disagree. And in the process we forget what we are fighting *about*—and both parties end up losers. What we need to learn are more sophisticated systems of *consensus argument,* in which the goal is seen not as a victory of one side over the other but as a mutually negotiated solution. Of course this involves admitting that the other side (that is, our "beloved spouse") may actually have something to say, and that we might profit from hearing it.

Communication is so crucial an aspect of intramarital growth that I will come back to it frequently in the book. Here I just want to suggest that essentially successful couples learn *metacommunicational* techniques to get around that old human tendency to close yourself off to all views but your own. Metacommunication involves learning to listen with the "third ear"—learning to set yourself outside the discussion, learning to talk about *how* you communicate as well as *what* you actually say. Such techniques can be learned, and they can markedly improve your chances of keeping even a troubled love relationship alive.

Change and Growth

The fundamental design behind developing all the above capacities is to help you learn to cope with change, and with the conflict that it often generates. I cannot stress too strongly the fact that change, far from being a "bad sign" within a relationship, can actually be the harbinger of enrichment and growth: as a result, it's those couples who can learn to deal with change rather than resist it who stand the best chance of seeing it re-create, and not destroy, the love they already have.

Since people are so radically individual, in personality and in history, it's never easy for two persons to live together. Even if you could somehow magically "freeze" time so that no external changes impinged on your relationship, conflict would still be inevitable, simply because the energies and expectations the two of you brought to the union in the first place could not possibly have formed a perfect fit. Unless you can succeed in turning yourselves into zombies, some degree of dissension, some sense of things being not quite right, is sure to characterize your life together. The trick in keeping your love alive is to see it not as a cause for despair but as an opportunity for developing new insights, new capacities for mutual growth, each time change starts battering at your door.

This is not simply making a virtue out of necessity. From a psychological point of view, change is absolutely necessary for growth; it is, in that sense, already a virtue. Without it, no relationship would ever go anywhere: we would remain moonstruck adolescents until the age of seventy-five, substituting billing and cooing and sweet nothings for the hard interactional energy that is the "real stuff" of a working union.

Sweet nothings, in short, are for kids. If you want to grow as a person, and if you want your partner to do the same, you have to begin looking at your relationship as an exciting but inherently difficult enterprise, one that needs care and a great deal of attention to make it flourish.

Giving it that attention is not easy, because we are trained to let love simply flow, as if, left to itself, it will always turn out for the best. What I hope this book will show you is that this kind of "hands off" attitude can be disastrous in human relationships. Children let things happen to them; it takes an adult to realize that he or she has control over what happens and can assume that control if he or she cares enough about the union.

Taking control is not an easy task, of course, because it involves taking responsibility as well—and that is something that many people, mired in self-recriminating dependency binds, choose not to do. But if you want your relationship to progress beyond the stage of puppy love, if you want to experience the real richness of a union of adults, you must take on responsibility for where the two of you are going. This means, of course, that you must stop blaming others (your spouse, your parents, your boss) for your troubles. I cannot deny, however, that doing so can be "scary as hell."

As we'll see throughout the rest of the book, though, it can also be one of the great rewards of interpersonal union.

Chapter 3

Great Expectations

Human beings thrive on hope. We also tend to cling to tradition, relying on old, accepted solutions rather than using our reasoning powers to develop new or different methods of problem solving. We may, for example, realize that electing a good or resourceful person to public office may have little or no effect on the machinery of government, but we continue to seek the perfect leader all the same. Similarly, marriages today may statistically have only a one-in-two chance of survival, but men and women continue to rush to the altar, hoping that they have chosen the "perfect" partner for life. But if we hope without a truly rational basis for our behavior, we do nothing more than adopt a philosophy of great expectations.

A philosophy of great expectations is easy to maintain and highly resilient. It can survive repeated failures, and leave you believing that a solution to your problems is still out there—in fact, if only you search harder, you'll probably find the solution to all your problems just around the corner.

Unfortunately, increased effort often sets the stage for more failure. A difficult fact to learn about personal accomplishment is that getting It (happiness, success, true love) frequently involves changing the very system of expectations that inspired the search for It in the first place.

Many romantic unions fail even before they begin simply because the parties involved enter them with a set of prescriptions to be filled, rather than with an open-minded willingness to allow the relationship to develop on its own. They ask for so much from the relationship that, even if it begins in real mutual affection, it founders because of the inability to meet the "tests" imposed on it by one or both hopeful partners. These tests can and often do serve as a way for inexperienced newlyweds to withdraw from a situation for which they have not been prepared.

Entering a relationship with a list of requirements almost always sets the stage for failure. I have seen this happen countless times with my patients, especially those who, despite their hopes for the relationship, actually anticipate that it will fail and therefore act defensively from the start—bringing about the very result they have feared. The fear of failure, in other words, can be a self-fulfilling prophecy.

All relationships have problems. The ones that succeed tend to be those in which the people involved accept their individual, and their mutual, limitations and consciously avoid the inclination to force their partners into preconceived roles. Working together to "make the best" of difficult situations will lead to healthier (and happier) results than committing yourself to a trouble-free, perfect relationship. Elaborate prescriptions, then, serve less as signposts than as traps.

Prescriptions

In the first chapter I considered how literary conventions, both medieval and modern, helped create a mythical view of romance as personally transforming, never changing, and ever new. These conventions, still alive today, continue to reflect and influence the way lovers look at relationships; they continue to raise false hopes about an extremely difficult and delicate human experience. The expectation that "true love" can change your life totally, and for good, has widespread effects in our culture even among people who have never read a Harlequin romance novel, and who would sneer at it if they had.

The expectation that romantic attachments in general, and marital unions in particular, will do something for you that you cannot, or will not, do for yourself creates major interpersonal problems. If you are not content to say to your partner, "I accept you and I hope you accept me," you are in effect imposing numerous demands on him (or her) that he very likely cannot meet.

As I pointed out in *Active Loving,* people tend to love *passively* rather than *actively,* and one reason for this is that they expect to *get* something from their love. Bound to dependency patterns in their relationships, they give of themselves only in the expectation of receiving something in return. This severely limits their real freedom as lovers, which is to be able to give without the expectation of return and to experience the joyous, self-enriching process of loving itself.

Often, when people marry, they tend to think of marriage as a final goal or objective, whose achievement has more significance for their happiness than the ongoing exchange of the feelings of affection and mutual esteem that led them to get married in the first place. When this happens, the institution takes over the emotion. Rather than helping people to learn to flow with the natural rhythms of intensive interaction, the culture links marriage to church and/or state rituals that officially sanction the relationship while at the same time reducing personal responsibility for its success. Thus the institution of marriage itself becomes part of what Marcia Seligson has called the Eternal Bliss Machine, imposing expectations and obligations on lovers that can actually undermine their natural feelings.*

Cultural prescription, rather than reflecting the ambivalence and fragility of human love, sets up both a code of good or acceptable behavior and a list of negative injunctions. Having done this, it defines a good union as one that adheres to the code, and a bad one as one that breaks it.

The code varies from time to time and from culture to culture. The notion that "real" lovers must follow prescribed rules (and roles) endures as does the idea that a failure to follow the code will lead to the death of the union. This notion informs not only the popular, silver-screen images of romance but many of the more scientific, academically respectable guides to success in loving that fill the paperback stands of our drugstores, supermarkets, and airports.

As Stanford psychologist Paul Watzlawick points out, however: "Few, if any, marriages live up to the ideals contained in the classic marriage manuals or popular mythology. Those who accept these ideas about what a mari-

*Marcia Seligson, *The Eternal Bliss Machine: the American Way of Wedding* (New York: Morrow, 1973).

tal relationship should 'really' be are likely to see their marriages as problematic and to start working towards its solution until divorce do them part."* The attempt to follow prescribed formulas for loving, then, can actually impede progress. Given the uniqueness of your life and your needs the choice of this or that "easy way" romantic formula will sooner or later leave you feeling "below par" and disappointed with the union. Only if you act on your own initiative, without regard to cultural demands, will you have a reasonable chance of developing a healthy relationship with another person.

In effect, the potential for success, whether in a romantic relationship or a business endeavor, lies within you, not outside of you. If you want to escape the traps into which half of all married couples fall today, you must first learn to *think for yourself* rather than leave it to the poets or the media. Only you can know what you want from a relationship, and only through your own experience can you determine the best ways to go about achieving what you want.

Take the case of Annette. Brought up to be a nurturing person like her mother, she invariably invited close relationships from dependent men who ignored her unique sense of self, and expected her to treat them in a way that did not correspond to her view of them. Such a sadomasochistic patterning invariably left her feeling depressed and angry, and resentful of the fact that she was being dumped on.

With therapy, she became more independent and found she could care for her own needs, and didn't need to rely on others; soon she experienced less disappoint-

*Paul Watzlawick, John Weakland, and Richard Fisch, *Change* (New York: Norton, 1974), p. 57.

ment and found she could focus on the real needs of her partners, develop more realistic expectations, and enjoy herself more in relationships.

Believing in the myth that "love conquers all" resembles buying a patent medicine that has not been prescribed for you personally and that probably will not be any more effective for your particular problem than any number of other patent medicines. To put it another way, *your* prescriptions must be specific to *your* needs.

To understand a little more clearly how people accept myths rather than think for themselves, consider one set of formulas to which a great many couples adhere: those social prescriptions that determine conventional sex roles.

Sex Roles and Rules

Anyone reading this book is probably all too painfully familiar with the conventional notions of masculine and feminine roles. The culture expects men to be cool, rational, hardworking, fearless, and protective; and women to be warm, intuitive, nurturing, timid, and irrational. Theoretically the ideal woman and man should form a perfect fit with each other, he providing the dominant, controlling elements of the relationship, she serving as his submissive "helpmate." This theory really functions as a source of friction and a constraint on human potential; that it seldom works out in reality can be observed in the divorce courts every day.

Psychologist Hogie Wyckoff in Claude Steiner's book *Scripts People Live,* observes:

> A particularly unhealthy result of our male-female sex role training is that gaps have been created in people which limit

their potential to become *whole* human beings. Often what happens with men and women is that they feel incomplete when they lack a partner of the opposite sex, so that they continually look for fulfillment in another . . . like two parts of a puzzle or two halves of a whole, men and women will often either direct their energy into looking for someone else to match up with and/or they will cling (fearfully) to an already established dependency relationship.*

The search does not always prove successful; the facility with which individuals today find Mr. or Miss Right, and then reject him or her in favor of someone "better," indicates the growing inability of traditional sex roles to meet the needs of today's flexible relationships. The rigid distinctions between housework and "real" work, between feeling and thinking, between "woman's place" and "man's place," may be viable, or at least operative, in certain traditional cultures. But in a culture like ours, where both internal and external change are so common, belief in strict male-female roles is only one more unrealistic expectation.

Even among traditional couples, where the man brings home the bacon and the woman puts it on the table, numerous unpredictable developments undermine the stability of the ideal. People who fit into the traditional sex roles today, therefore, frequently do so by *repressing* aspects of their personalities instead of *expressing* them. The wife who refuses a part-time job because her husband doesn't want her to work, or the husband who cannot hug his own son because men "don't do such things" are trying to adhere to external standards rather than fill their own prescriptions. This can have disastrous results for a relationship, even if the surface looks smooth.

*In Claude Steiner, *Scripts People Live* (New York: Bantam, 1975), p. 197.

Take the recent movie *Norma Rae,* for example. One of its major subplots concerns the heroine's relationship with her husband, Sonny. Newly married, they experience only minor differences of opinion until Norma Rae begins working with labor organizer Ruben Warshavsky and neglects her "wifely duties." In spite of the absence of any sexual involvement with Ruben, their friendship troubles Sonny simply because it threatens his concept of marriage, in which the wife (even though she holds a full-time job) must handle the cooking, cleaning, laundry, and childcare.

This type of marital situation, increasingly common, illustrates the dissension that can arise when changing circumstances disrupt a couple's "prescribed" mode of behavior. Conventional cultural norms led Sonny to expect that Norma Rae would continue to fulfill her "wifely duties" irrespective of other commitments. Her refusal to follow his prescriptions of appropriate behavior led to a state of conflict that ended only when its source, the "outside agitator," left town.

Itinerant labor organizers threaten relatively few marriages today. Many marriages, however, have to contend with evolving notions of male and female marital roles, and a surprisingly small number of them manage to meet the difficulties involved in sex-role division. As a result, a social development that might have breathed new life into modern marriages seems—so far—to have contributed to their instability. Because couples refuse to modify their role expectations of husbands and wives, they end up unable to adjust to changes brought about by a rapidly evolving social matrix—and rather than change their rules, they break apart.

Wyckoff describes the conflict often brought about by

what he calls the Sex Role Conspiracy—a "conspiracy" he blames for causing the problems it should have resolved:

> There's a mystification about the way men and women are scripted to go together like sweet and sour sauce, hot and cold, *yin* and *yang*. It's supposedly a groovy, beautiful thing. The problem is that people don't fit together very well that way. . . . Actually, it is in this way that men and women become mysteries to each other, rather than complements. . . . And as far as relationships go, believing the myth of complementary sex roles conspires against genuine success because communication between men and women is broken down in so many ways.*

Relying on your own instincts can be difficult in a culture that characterizes "real" men as "tough hombres" who never cry and "real" women as tantalizingly sensual and aromatic "10s" who never sweat. As ludicrous and farfetched as they may be, the images of sex roles and behavior in perfume and beer commercials create powerful prescriptive models for the way people should act in "real" life. People become dissatisfied—unconsciously usually—because neither they nor their partners measure up to the media images.

To avoid the trap of unrealistic expectations, try to remember that nobody "out there"—not a perfume commercial, not a book, and not even a beloved spouse—can tell you how things "should" be in your relationships. You must learn to *think for yourself*.

Remember, also, that your spouse will be thinking, too —and no one can guarantee that the two of you will reach the same or even similar solutions to your mutual problems. Solutions, like expectations, invariably *diverge*.

Ibid, pp. 205–206.

Diverging Expectations

In an "ideal" romantic union, the two parties enter the relationship with identical expectations about behavior and roles; nothing ever disturbs these expectations, and the two live happily ever after.

In actual fact, the expectations people bring to marriage seldom materialize in the day-to-day development of the relationship, and rarely, if ever, do *the two sets of expectations of both partners coincide.*

Even Sonny and Norma Rae, who were raised in the same mill town, experienced conflict because their expectations and needs began to differ. Think how much more divergent the expectations and needs of people from quite different backgrounds can be. Remember, too, the crucial effects of family history, birth order, established behavior patterns, and personality on any human interaction.

It's easy to forget the importance of divergence when you feel at one with your partner—especially in the early stages of relationships. Infatuation can be so great that it brings together people with radically different hopes for their lives; since few infatuated couples go to the trouble of plotting out a step-by-step Life Plan early on, a large percentage of these "mismatched" unions don't work out.

Given the number of personal and social variables that go to make up any individual personality, it sometimes seems amazing that any two people can ever get along at all. Consider the potential social, educational, cultural, ethnic, sexual, religious, and family differences between any two people and you'll realize how many ways in which true lovers, once they start living together, can clash. For every moonlit inspiration they may experience together, they also bring to the relationship a host of quite specific expectations that can eclipse the moonlight in an instant.

Each person has a basic repertoire of attitudes, values, and patterns of behavior that he or she learned as a child in relation to siblings, parents, teachers, and peers. These experiences create characteristic ways of relating to others, and become part and parcel of the personality. As a relationship evolves, partners tend to react to and reinforce the habits and patterns most familiar to them, thereby re-creating a world like the one they knew as children—even when that world may seem uncomfortable and disruptive to an outsider. Naturally, no two childhood worlds will ever match perfectly, and so conflict between two people inevitably occurs.

Commonly, people encountering a clash of different values or expectations try to impose their own standards on one another. The results are predictable. The attempt to transform your partner's view of the world by shouting "My way is the right way" very seldom leads to anything but increased misunderstanding, polarization, and anger.

For this reason, some couples, to keep the peace, resort to conciliatory tactics and go along with their spouses instead of fighting. Unfortunately, such tactics can be even worse than outright confrontations. Stifling oneself in order to keep the peace does not necessarily placate others. It may be construed as a passively hostile act, and it may evoke a sense of inadequacy and insecurity. In addition, if you go along with another's expectations of how things "ought" to be done, you yourself may experience resentment, guilt, and destructive tension.

One of my patients, for example, used to go along with

his wife's rather halfhearted suggestion that he accompany her to the supermarket out of a sense of duty. Hearing her suggestion as a command, he would go along even though he hated shopping. "While waiting for her to finish," he explained to me, "I'd be burning. I'd park somewhere in the forty-minute zone, wait for her to load up the packages and stew until one comment from me about being there would set her off like a Roman candle." He was a perfect case of someone willfully repressing his own needs to meet someone else's imagined expectations. Actually, therapy revealed that his wife really preferred shopping alone anyway, and had only been asking him to go along out of a distorted view of *his* expectations! In trying to please each other at all costs, both of them had been suffering unnecessarily.

In effect, their great expectations led to an almost symmetrical competition, each trying to outdo the other in "pleasing" behavior until they had increased the mutual pressure to the point of exhaustion. Only when they had come to grips with their individual needs, rather than their distorted views of the other person's needs, did their relationship begin to blossom.

To break free of unrealistic expectations, you must learn to think for yourself. It's true that in the best of relationships you also must learn to think for your partner, but this doesn't mean mind-reading or compliance with what you think your spouse expects of you; that can have the same negative effect as a confrontation. When, instead of working out a mutually satisfactory resolution to your difficulties, you "go along" with your own distorted perceptions of your partner's expectations, suppressed resentment can build to an intolerable level. At this point it explodes in confrontation only to be followed by feelings of guilt and contrition. In turn, this leads to more compliance and again a buildup of resentment.

You want to aim for a situation in which your needs are balanced against your spouse's needs and against those of the relationship as a whole. Before achieving that kind of balance, of course, you first have to know your individual and mutual needs and learn to share them with each other, clearly and without hostility.

Few couples do this, either at the outset of their relationship or periodically when most needed. Assuming they have met their expectations and needs when in fact they actually have only ignored tensions, many couples live with each other for years without ever expressing their feelings.

Many couples, in other words, fail to acknowledge that their expectations have diverged, and proceed on the erroneous assumption that without conflict there are no problems. They live "as if" things were going as they wanted.

Living "As If"

At the beginning of the movie *Kramer vs. Kramer*, the energetic advertising man Ted Kramer comes home to announce to his wife that he has just been handed a major account. Jubilant and eager to celebrate, he dances through the door, pecks her on the cheek, and makes a quick business call. Then, turning around to tell her the good news, he discovers that she has news for him: her bags are packed, and she's leaving him. "This is some kind of a joke," he protests as the elevator door closes. It has come as a total surprise.

Now, as the movie makes clear, the signs of trouble

between the Kramers had been there for some time. Too
preoccupied with his work, Ted failed to notice that his
wife had been getting increasingly distant and depressed.
In fact she had frequently, mostly in nonverbal ways, sol-
icited his help and attention, but he had shut her out,
preferring to believe that things were going along fine.
Her decision to leave, then, has to be seen not as the
capricious act of an unstable woman—which is how he
ultimately interprets it—but as the desperate and inevitable final solution to a situation in which *communication
has broken down.* Ted responds in a typical fashion for
someone in his situation: he refuses to see how things
could have gotten so bad, because he had not been looking at them for some time.

The kind of confusion illustrated by the Kramers' situation commonly results from crossed signals or blocked
lines of communication. In a way it can be seen as the
ultimate result of differing expectations, when one party,
unwilling to acknowledge that his hopes and his spouse's
have diverged, behaves *as if they have not*—and thus
ensures that the recognition of diversity, when it comes,
will be all the more abrupt and painful.

While his wife tries to voice her own needs, Ted ignores
them and proceeds *as if* his own vision were complete,
and his own interpretation were reality. His expectation
that she will rejoice with him at his good fortune has
therefore both a poignant and a ridiculous quality. While
the relationship has been changing under his nose, he has
kept his eye on a myth—a sad, and all too typical, example
of the blindness of love.

Living "as if" an expectation were being met instead of
being undermined is an example of those "terrible simplifications" that Paul Watzlawick has identified as a "crit-

ical interactional impasse." According to Watzlawick, in many relationships it's not the observable problem itself (silence, infidelity, money) that breaks the couple up, but the *denial that the problem exists.* The problem is only made worse when the partner who denies the problem asserts that the other partner is "mad or bad" for pointing it out.* This refusal to acknowledge the validity of your partner's (divergent) views has been called "discounting" by British psychologist R. D. Laing. As Ted's case shows, it can lead to the very thing that willful denial of the problem had blocked out.

Ted's problem was primarily one of a lack of communication. But problems can arise even when both partners do talk. A great many problems arise from misperception and misinterpretation—from seeing anger, for example, as evidence of hostility when it may actually represent an automatic defensive response. In an argument expression of anger is a mechanism that takes the place of shared perceptions, and prevents you from dealing forthrightly with the problem.

Laura Huxley, the writer Aldous Huxley's wife, discovered this in the last years of their life together. Through much anguish and self-examination, she came to realize that her husband's frequent tirades against her, as he lay dying of cancer, disguised his own thwarted expectations, and were not meant as personal attacks on her. Understanding that helped her to be less defensive and less hurt when he exploded, and helped her to realize the truth, which she incorporated into the title of her memoir: *You Are Not the Target.*

The other person's expectations, in other words, count

*Watzlawick et al., *Change,* chapter 4.

as much as your own in determining how to adapt to mutual needs. Like Laura Huxley, you must make a calm, balanced appraisal of how your needs both overlap and diverge—and on top of that you must develop a willingness to embrace the difficult task of communication to see if your needs can in some way be brought into concert with each other.

Misperceptions, of course, occur more often than communication. For this reason, the parties involved in any loving relationship must be willing first to *recognize* their differences and then to *negotiate* common grounds. Learning to listen is one of the first steps in doing this.

The Self-fulfilling Prophecy

The title of a once popular play suggests how lovers frequently cut themselves off from the opportunity to listen to each other. The play *I Can't Hear You When the Water's Running* concerned the misadventures of a young couple who could not hear each other talking above the sounds of the bathtub being filled with water. The central motif illustrates a common communication problem. Consider, if you will, the image of the wife or husband standing exasperated outside a closed bathroom door, yelling to the spouse inside, who can't hear a word being said. It's an extreme but illustrative metaphor for what goes on every day in many relationships.

Even in the best of circumstances, communication can be difficult. Communication comprises spoken and unspoken messages, objective data and subjective nuance, specific information and nonspecific instructions about how the information is to be handled. How you say it sometimes matters more than what you say.

Take the case of Beverly. Married for eighteen years to her childhood sweetheart, she always assumed that she and her husband knew each other's needs, but never once expressed her own needs in terms of her feelings. Rather than tell Ben about her frustration and fatigue and asking him to help her, she elected to chide him for "making a mess" about the house, and resigned herself to the belief that "he would never learn." Only as she became aware of her own dependency needs, the value of communicating her feelings, and the negative impact of her bossy style—only, that is, by stepping outside the system—could she begin to change the nature of her marital relationship.

The complexity of communication makes some misunderstandings inevitable, and this is all the more reason you must consciously try to sit quietly and listen to what others have to say, rather than react automatically by throwing up personal defenses and relying on anger, second-guessing, and aired grievances. Contrary to common belief, communication does not improve with increased volume. Barry !!!

The *anticipation of incomprehension* plays a major part in most interactions. Expecting to be "rejected" by others, you may interpret the slightest disagreement as an outright, full-fledged denial. Or, anticipating that your lover will think badly of you if you say what's really on your mind, you clam up, feel guilty, retreat—and end up eliciting the very reaction that you had intended to avoid. Rather than engage in a real interchange with each other, you repeatedly set yourself up to be disappointed—and then say "I told you so" when your prophecies are fulfilled.

The reason for this self-fulfilling process relates to what I said earlier about great expectations being a design for failure. As much as you may like to believe that your high hopes for the future of your union reflect optimism, in many cases they indicate just the opposite. *Going into a relationship expecting it to be perfect ensures that you will be able to get out of it easily when it proves to be something less than ideal.* In the same way you may use the inevitable misunderstandings in daily interaction not as a spur to improvement but as proof that "things can never work out" between you as long as friction exists. Expecting to be unsuccessful, you get just what you ask for.

Psychologically, this can be very comforting—or at least easier to take than honestly opening yourself up to your partner and letting him or her know what's bothering you. If you secretly anticipate the worst, you can avoid the anxiety of letting another person know, "Hey, I hurt, I'm lonely, I don't want to be rejected." If you say "things will be wonderful" and think "things will be lousy," you never have to make those admissions: the destruction of the relationship can be seen as something that happens, just like the Perfect Marriage, "out there."

By cherishing false expectations, you can hold on to the illusion of independence even while you remain enmeshed in a supposedly mutual enterprise. Wishing for the best while expecting the worst becomes a way both of reinforcing romantic illusions and of ensuring that a particular union can never live up to those illusions. This structure of false hopes and hidden dependencies explains why half of all relationships fail.

Can you escape this negative scenario? Can you learn to communicate honestly? Can you do more than shadow dance with those you love?

Yes. You and your partner can learn various techniques

to open the lines of communication between you. Briefly stated, enhanced communication requires two basic skills: (1) the ability to say what you mean in a nonabrasive manner, and (2) the ability to listen to what the other person is saying without reacting defensively.

To say what you mean, you have to learn to identify and acknowledge your feelings without fear of being "attacked" and without "blaming" your spouse for those feelings. In the same way, you can only begin to listen to what your spouse has to say if you remember that expectations diverge, and that your spouse's emotional responses may not coincide with yours. Recognizing this, you'll be in a better position to listen to what he or she has to say without overreacting to disagreeable views.

The difficult skill of learning to talk with each other is essential for a healthy union. If you can openly express your own feelings as well as listen to your partner's expression of feelings, you will improve mutual understanding and trust and increase the intensity of the relationship. If you only reluctantly speak about sensitive subjects for fear of hurting your partner's feelings, or if you hear every thoughtless thing he or she says as an attack on you, you will find yourself engaged in a series of manipulations that create anxiety, tension, and resentment.

You can't be open just once and then quit. You and your partner can benefit from *periodically* trying to clarify your expectations about your relationship and about your respective roles. Misunderstandings about these roles can lead to confusion about the interactions that grow out of them, and this in turn can lead to resistance, defensiveness, and progressively increasing conflict.

You may make the assumption that your partner should know exactly what you want without being briefed periodically by you. This unrealistic belief is based on the notion that you and your partner are one rather than distinct and complex individuals. No doubt you have shared close moments when the boundaries between you seem to have melted, but that is not going to be a day-to-day reality. Only if you can accept your distinct uniqueness will you be able to clarify, and communicate, your expectations. This means accepting the fact that the two of you are not one.

This is the lovers' paradox: the more you can accept each other as being *autonomous,* the better your *mutuality* will be. In effect, to reduce the impact of great expectations you must both recognize that you have them. Recognizing this fact will enable you to step outside the frame of reference of the relationship itself, with its established interaction sequences, so as to be able to improve the quality of communication.

Because most people fail to listen to one another, they view conflict as the fault of the other rather than as part of an interactional system. But it takes two to tangle. Attributing your conflicts to the other person's failure to live up to your expectations too often tragically leads to the breakdown of communication, and the breakdown of close unions themselves.

In fact nobody can ever live up to your expectations—a lesson too few learn early enough to benefit their shaky unions. Assuming conflict to be the other person's fault, they hear only what they want to hear, criticize each other, and end up separated indefinitely by insurmountable communication barriers.

Chapter 4

Two to Tangle

The first time I saw John he expressed an ambivalence about his wife, Lucille. "I don't understand why I have such mixed feelings about her," he said. "I can't live with her and I can't live without her."

I explained to him that such mixed feelings were a normal response to the natural flow of relationships. The shifts in any relationship from intimacy to separation and back again are bound to create contradictory feelings and make confusion inevitable.

John still looked confused, so I outlined the changes that were likely to occur in the course of a relationship that would cause conflict and mixed emotions.

Some changes, I said, occur as the result of *external* factors such as the Critical Life Events measured by Drs. Holmes and Rahe—events like births, deaths, divorce, and changes of residence and occupation.* No matter how firm a commitment you and your spouse may have, these events can create tension between you.

Other changes result from *individual* experiences in response to both internal and external influences. The

*T. H. Holmes and R. H. Rahe, "The Social Readjustment Rating Scale," *Journal of Psychosomatic Research* 11 (1967):213–218.

development of a new and time-consuming interest, dissatisfaction with your employment, a radical change in health—these kinds of things can have immediate and profound influences on how you view your relationship—and thus on how it evolves.

Finally, *collective* changes occur as a direct result of the fact that you are part of a "couple." Relationships create their own context for change—as well as for conflict. When you consider the differences between two people and the complexity of relationships, it's not surprising to find even very close-knit unions intermittently troubled by conflict. A kind of internal up-and-down rhythm of conflict and change can be observed, in fact, in almost all relationships. The inevitability of collective change results from the fact that two people in a relationship usually build up an automatic tension between their need to be together and their need to be alone as they become closer to each other. This chapter focuses on the management of that tension.

The Push-Pull of Relationships

The case of John and Lucille illustrates how hard it can be to maintain the fundamental balance of romantic union: the balance between togetherness and aloneness, or what I prefer to call *mutuality* and *autonomy*. Despite their genuine fondness of each other, they could not relate to each other for long without some evidence of dissension. This dissension evolved in a predictable, recurrent pattern, almost as if it were scripted:

1. Lucille demanded more attention from John than he could give to her. Unwilling to respond to her demands,

John retreated completely into himself and gave her even less attention than before.

2. Realizing that she would lose John by her persistent demands for closeness, Lucille shifted to being distraught, teary-eyed, and apologetic.

3. This brought John rushing back. But once they were close again, Lucille invariably would ask him, "Do you love me?" He would respond, "Of course." She would then berate him for never showing it enough.

4. Interpreting this criticism as a renewed demand for closeness, John would retreat again—thus beginning the whole cycle over again.

John and Lucille had created a familiar scenario, an *interpersonal bind* in which one partner's need for togetherness evoked precisely the opposite need in the other, driving the two apart until they reached a nervous equilibrium and could come together again, only to repeat the pattern. This pattern occurs with great regularity in many relationships.

The seemingly contradictory needs for solitude and for social contact makes inevitable the push-pull aspect of close unions. Afraid of being entirely alone, people seek out partners who will help them to face the void; but being wary of intimacy, or real union, they periodically conspire with themselves and with their mates to maintain a certain distance between them and thus sustain the conviction of their separate selves.

Couples are two, and they are one. This paradox, which is at the heart of all close relationships, illustrates our dual needs for *dependence* and *independence*. If you are like most people, you no doubt feel the need to pursue your own star without worrying about the needs of others; and you also feel the need to rely on those others for support and comfort when the star-chasing gets lonely. You want to have it both ways, and yet you can accomplish that only by means of a constant push and pull, or what Gail Sheehy calls the "yo-yo syndrome" of alternately favoring the "Merger Self" and the "Seeker Self."* The tension between these two selves, as she notes, provides a basic context for interpersonal disagreement from childhood straight into old age.

If you've been in a close union, you'll recognize what she's talking about. But you may not understand its psychological significance.

Why does this uneasy push-pull occur? Generally, the roots of the movement back and forth between mutuality and autonomy lie in childhood experiences of rejection or separation.

In Lucille's case, it resulted from her deep and ultimately unsatisfied love for her father, who she felt rejected her in favor of her mother. As a child she had been very close to her father, but could not maintain this closeness through adolescence. By keeping John at a distance, she was able to re-experience the old familiar feeling of partial rejection and at the same time avoid the intimacy that she feared would lead to "total abandonment." She set herself up for a situation in which her expectations of incompletion were met in the same ambivalent way they were met when she was a child.

Such patterns pervade our culture. In most cases, the people who fear rejection the most do the most to ensure that it will occur. Like Lucille, they become so anxious about a developing intimacy (which they see as a prelude

*Gail Sheehy, *Passages: Predictable Crises of Adult Life* (New York: Dutton, © 1976).

to abandonment), they begin to behave in a controlling, possessive, demanding manner, ostensibly to achieve intimacy, but actually to ensure that they don't. Thus they fulfill their own dire prediction.

Other times, people try to behave more decently, more cautiously, so that they don't "scare the other person away." Ironically, this usually only ensures that separation and distance remain constant aspects of their relationships. Because they fear being hurt (that is, being abandoned), if they get too close to another individual, they opt for a respectable distance, and allow themselves to stay "half-abandoned" all the time. Only when they feel themselves starting to get really frozen out of a relationship do they begin to demand closeness intently: many times, in situations like this, they act like Lucille, and end up driving their partner away.

You can see the repetitive, almost compulsive nature of the push-pull and how it actually serves to aggravate the very anxiety over separation it might have alleviated.

In some instances, the conflict between mutuality and autonomy creates such intolerable tensions as to lead to actual physical separation. In one couple I counseled, both husband and wife became locked into a pattern of mutual criticism. Peggy regularly invited criticism from Phil by asking his approval for decisions she had already made. Phil usually complied with the head-shaking resentment he knew she expected in response.

At the same time, Phil encouraged Peggy to make decisions without consulting him, because this enhanced his self-image as the spouse of a smart, active woman. He enjoyed this arrangement until she began to take him up on his demand that she "do more things by herself," because this actually made him more insecure: when he saw

*impassive
indiff.
non complaining*

her becoming really autonomous, he became critical of her activities. Feeling overburdened and guilty, she then began to make efforts to "break free." Not wanting to show his dependency, Phil adopted an attitude of stoic indifference. Peggy interpreted this as real indifference, then as rejection, and left him to make a new life for herself in California.

But—and here is the crucial point—as soon as they separated and her need for autonomy was fulfilled, her need for closeness and intimacy surfaced and she became anxious and depressed without him. After much consideration, she decided to return to him. It wasn't so much independence that she had craved as it was a healthier balance between the demands of her Seeker and Merger selves. But she, like many people, could achieve that balance only by going first in one direction, then in another.

The Ideal Interpersonal Space

The push-pull between people has some of the characteristics of the attraction and repulsion of magnets. You may remember the little bar magnets you used to play with in grade school. Like all magnets they were charged with a negative pole and a positive pole. If you put the positive pole of one magnet next to the positive pole of another, the two would repel each other. The same thing would happen if you placed two negative poles together. Only when you put the positive end of one magnet next to the negative end of the other would you get that "click" of metal on metal that told you their force fields had merged.

The analogy with human beings is instructive, though limited. Like magnets, you have a positive pole (the need for togetherness, or intimacy) and a negative pole (the need for autonomy, or separateness). The push-pull between you reflects a kind of interactional force field now attracting, now repelling, as you turn in various directions in your life.

But your "charges" are far more complicated and changeable than the fixed, predictable charges of a magnet. Putting a magnet's positive pole next to another magnet's negative pole always results in union. This does not occur with human beings. While the idea that opposites attract works as a rule of thumb for magnets, it works only some of the time for humans; the rest of the time the rules seem reversed, and human force fields run according to "like attracting like."

Another way of looking at this would be to imagine that your attraction to and repulsion from those you love stems from an interactional system of fluctuating rather than fixed charges. The fluctuation, moreover, seems to be regulated by the interaction itself, and not simply by the whims of one or another partner. Lucille's strong positive demands led Jack to "repel" her; just as her distance from him restored the "attraction" between them. So for human "magnets," getting close to one another in itself alters the rules of attraction and repulsion.

It's as if all couples were somehow working toward an ideal interpersonal space—one that would satisfy their particular needs and no others—by moving away as soon as they got close, and moving together again as soon as some distance had been gained. Jockeying back and forth, then, between too far and too close might be seen not as an unpleasant dilemma, but as a mode of constant redefinition.

But can there be such a thing as an ideal interpersonal space?

Consider the question purely from a physical standpoint. What constitutes the ideal distance between two people engaged in a friendly conversation? Should they stand three feet apart? Three inches? Three yards?

The question may seem a bit silly, but actually every culture has its own well-defined notion of the ideal physical distance for various situations. Arabs, for example, like to discuss things almost cheek to cheek as it were—yet if you tried to stand that close to a Swiss or an American, he would think of you as intrusive. If you maintained a "proper" distance from an Egyptian friend, on the other hand, you would be accused of coolness.

Given such a variety of opinions on the proper physical space to maintain between acquaintances, you can imagine how complicated the issue becomes when you consider psychological space. You may know exactly how far your spouse wants your face to be from hers when you talk, but that won't help you determine how far away she'd like your emotions. That's a much more tenuous and much more frequently shifting thing to measure—but just as important. In addition, just as internal needs and desires change, so too will the distance you perceive as ideal between you.

Patterns of distancing take even more dramatic forms in matters of territoriality. You may be familiar with the "fight or flight" response elicited in a dog, for example, as you pass his yard. To defend his ideal space, he'll rush up to the fence, growl at you, and threaten you with bared teeth if you dare to come too close—but then, once he has chased you from his territory onto your own turf, he will retreat from you if you make a move in his direction. In other words, your movements are reciprocal—his forward motion determines your backward motion, but only up to the point where he invades "your" space. This goes on in many fish species as well, with individual fish battling over an imaginary line between them until a nervous equilibrium is reached.

Humans in close relationships perform somewhat the same kind of dance. As one member of a relationship attempts to move closer, the other, feeling threatened by the anticipation of the rejection that so often follows intimacy, frequently backs off. This may offend the first person, who may back off in turn, thus setting up a psychological distance between them and, not uncommonly, causing the second person to make the next move forward.

It can be pretty frustrating if you keep trying to achieve a permanent perfect balance between mutuality and autonomy. It's unlikely that this will ever occur. In fact, nothing ever remains the same for long in relationships. The quest for the perfect balance of oneness and twoness proves ultimately to be just as futile as the quest for the perfect partner.

This doesn't mean that balance can't be achieved, however, or that you will always be at the mercy of unpredictable forces. On the contrary; in spite of the numerous internal variables of individual psychology, there do seem to be some fairly consistent patterns of personal interaction, and getting in touch with them can make your experience in a "one plus one" union a lot easier.

These patterns, as they develop over time, may be grouped into three basic phases.

The Three Phases of Relationships

The changing nature of personal objectives forever complicates the process of achieving the right balance between closeness and separateness. I've described the continual flux that characterizes relationships, and that makes it impossible to establish a balance that will remain appropriate and set for all time. However, you can hope to develop enough sensibility about your own needs, and those of your partner, to be able to anticipate and manage friction when it arises. If you're in a close union, the tension between autonomy and mutuality will shift inevitably no matter what you do about it. Luckily, these shifts don't occur randomly, but follow a definite sequence of phases that recur at intervals.

Most relationships, as I have mentioned previously, pass again and again through the following three phases: the phase of *approach*, or developing intimacy; the phase of *unity*, or intense mutual support; and the phase of *separation*, dominated by the need for autonomy. These phases operate in a cyclical rather than linear fashion, so that the separation phase typically leads back to the approach phase, thus starting the whole cycle over again.

All three phases have their place in a healthy, developing relationship; in the best relationships, couples learn from practice how to flow naturally from separation to intimacy and back again—neither fearing the one nor clinging to the other. Moreover, they learn how to weather the conflict involved in the transition from one phase to another.

Now, problems usually surface between phases, and this can disguise the fact that intimacy, no less than separation, can be a source of turmoil. Indeed, *all* phases of a relationship have their troubles, despite the conventional romantic wisdom that problems in a loving union reflect the breakdown of intimacy, and that true mutuality means being entirely free of anxiety.

The approach phase, in fact, can be a terrifying experience. When you first become involved with another person, you not only surrender your individual quirks and ways of doing things, but you also open yourself and make yourself vulnerable to someone who is still something of a stranger. Many potential unions never get past the approach phase simply because one or both parties fear deeply the feelings of vulnerability and the anticipation of rejection associated with developing intimacy.

So, a kind of anticipatory fear often accompanies the excitement of "falling in love." Most people fear losing their identity to interpersonal involvement. This holds especially true for independent individuals and those struggling to become independent. They resist what they want to obtain. They undermine themselves at the outset, holding back lest they be "swallowed up" by love.

This can be a healthy response. As long as the reluctance to acknowledge growing intimacy does not get "frozen" into a permanent attitude—as long as caution does not turn into an obstacle to any commitment—there may be a good purpose served by going a little slow at the start. Many unions falter because one person, fearing rejection, forces or rushes the approach phase, trying to establish the phase of union before his or her partner is ready. Since intimacy may activate dormant fears of separation, a new union should be allowed to develop at its own casual pace. Attempts to consolidate unity too rapidly can lead to conflict and defensive avoidance. Shortcuts to bliss, in other words, can turn into short circuits.

Unable to tolerate uncertainty and feeling pressured by the fact that her child-bearing years were coming to an end, Kathy, a thirty-four-year-old loan officer, pushed too hard for commitment from Steve, her boyfriend of six months. His reluctance to commit himself to her stemmed in part from his reaction to her pressure, not from a lack of positive feeling. Fearing that the relationship might fail, she anxiously set in motion a negative self-fulfilling prophecy: she pressed for intimacy so strongly that the results were confrontations, ultimatums, and the dissolution of the relationship. The union might have succeeded if Kathy and Steve had explored their respective feelings calmly and with an understanding of their different needs and expectations; as it was, "too much too soon" spelled defeat.

Ambivalence about a partner, and about the wisdom of intimacy, can also carry over into the *unity* phase. I see this often in newly married couples who, to disguise their own uncertainties about marriage, become inseparable, expressing an intolerance for being apart. While this may look wonderful, it can be problematic. Sometimes the couples who seem closely knit are actually in deep trouble. Failing to recognize their individual needs for autonomy—even while they're coming together—can lead to suppressed resentment, guilt, and an intensification of the desire to get away. Although this can be handled easily by talking about it, many couples, afraid to air their own ambivalent feelings, cling more tightly together when they feel uncertain, ignoring their growing feelings of emptiness and boredom until these tear the union apart.

Strong feelings of intimacy, then, often evoke uncomfortable feelings of dependency and vulnerability. You and your partner may derive strength from each other, but you may also experience conflict because of an unwillingness to be open to that dependency—and to the negative sensations associated with it. Rather than risk the loss of a relationship, you may exaggerate the positive feelings you have about each other and suppress expressions of autonomy that might suggest that you do not accept complete oneness. Such suppression and denial may seem comforting on the surface, but eventually they will distort your perception of each other, and of the union itself.

This can happen even quite late in a relationship, as it shifts from the initial romantic stage to the "daily living" stage, with its numerous practical concerns. The early idealization of your partner may lessen as your attention to the problems of daily living increases. This may heighten your partner's dependency demands on you, creating in you feelings of being stifled and having your "ideal space" disrupted. This may cause you to move apart from your partner—leaving both of you with feelings of abandonment.

Each phase, then, has its own problems, and if you are not diligent about monitoring your feelings and sharing them with each other, the problems of one phase can easily lead to a vicious cycle of increasingly defensive and conflict-ridden behavior.

Stages of Evolution

I hope I have made it clear that the cyclical progression of phases goes on constantly throughout a relationship. Like the turning yin-yang symbol, each of the two basic elements of the relationship, mutuality and autonomy, has some of its opposite within it. The need for independence continually intrudes on the approach phase, and lovers retain a strong sense of mutual attraction in the separation phase. You cannot, therefore, think of the three phases as clearly defined segments of a line: like the life of the relationship itself, they constantly shift gears, speed up or slow down, trade off, and battle for equilibrium.

Yet the motion is not entirely unpredictable. Certain stages in the life cycle accentuate the drive for autonomy, while other stages foster patterns of mutuality. Because of this, it is possible to some extent to anticipate whether mutuality or autonomy will predominate during a given period. Thus, in addition to daily, weekly, and seasonal phase shifts, you can expect an overall pattern of life *stages* that goes something like this:

- In the first ten years of the relationship, you as a couple will focus most of your energy on approach, trying to establish close contact with each other in the exciting exploration of intimacy.

- In the second ten years of the relationship, provided you have been successful in establishing a successful level of intimacy and mutuality, you'll probably spend most of your energy on togetherness—at times to the point of stifling your personal creative endeavors. If you have not been successful, these years may be characterized by considerable conflict, mutual manipulation, or a general pattern of avoidance as ways of coping with excessive togetherness.

- In the third ten years of the relationship, you will probably begin to make efforts to break free of the constraints of union, and to find a newly personalized sense of self. The shift away from union and toward separation frequently accompanies the so-called mid-life crisis, when your children become more independent, leaving you time to examine where you've come so far. The successful couple will obviously weather this stage with fewer disruptions, separations, and major crises than the couple that has been moving in the direction of greater overt or covert dissension.

- If you weather the "storm" created by this re-examination, the next decade or two will be characterized by an increasing sense of closeness and mutuality, and ultimately an increasing dependency in the last years of your marriage. The need for autonomy often gets "burned out" in the mid-life crisis, so that couples in their fifties and sixties frequently exhibit a closer sense of togetherness than people at any younger age. Obviously those that don't weather the storm are most likely either to break up during this stage or to reach a rather uneven and conflict-ridden adaptation.

But no one can guarantee you that this pattern will match your individual development patterns. The broad perspective suggests that people in their fifties tend to move closer together, but if you have been repressing your own sense of autonomy on a daily basis for thirty years before that, you may find your hidden needs exploding at age fifty, leading you to go winging off to California to find a new, unrepressed self.

Friction often arises at such times. The general pattern may be one of approach-union-autonomy-approach, but since no two people will go through this lifelong cycle at precisely the same rate of change, you and your partner can get badly "out of synch" with each other, both on a day-to-day and on a longer-term basis. Fortunately, friction such as this does not have to result in disaster but can be the basis for actually strengthening your relationship.

Progression and Growth

People seldom develop at the same rate of change. You cannot count on your lover to remain fixed in perfect harmony with you forever no matter how "in tune" you have been at the outset of your relationship. Inevitably, as you both grow and encounter new experiences, the push-pull of mutuality and autonomy will work differently on the two of you, and you'll find yourself running into missed beats, erratic tempos, and discord.

Later on we'll consider the resolution of specific instances of interpersonal discord. Here I want to emphasize the fact that, properly managed, *discord can actually enrich rather than diminish your love.*

More often than not, the couples who have been out of synch with each other have adapted best to their situation by confronting their difficulties rather than avoiding or ignoring them. Those who have prospered most have absorbed the discord into their relationship and made it part of the basis for healthy change. Those who have failed to survive their difficulties have been those who have refused to acknowledge that they could learn about themselves from those difficulties.

Growth in a relationship depends not on sameness but, ironically, on unevenness: on variety and mutation and trouble. Human beings, like other dynamic and living beings, actually profit from disequilibrium and discomfort, because these provide the tension so necessary for generating healthy levels of activity, flexibility, and interest. Without such tension people tend to become complacent or bored very quickly. It may seem comfortable to find a niche and live out each day expecting it to be exactly like the last, but this can be disastrous for relationships. Close unions need stimulation for their survival.

This means that in a long-term relationship you must develop the capacity to handle change over time, to accept it as inevitable (and inevitably confusing), and then to incorporate it into the interaction that has generated it—and on which it depends. For without that capacity, couples generally fall into the trap of *illusory permanence* —living as if their relationship existed without phases, without stages, and without development. Only in fairy tales would this situation be considered desirable—or even conceivable.

You may be familiar with the post-honeymoon syndrome: that feeling of boredom and uselessness that wells up right after the initial rush of the approach phase has passed. Many newlyweds can weather this transitional syndrome, though some—convinced that all the change is bad—scurry to the divorce court the minute they feel the least bit out of synch. Rather than viewing dissension as a spur to progress, they regress to dreaming about How Wonderful Things Used To Be, and end up destroying the union. Successful loving couples, on the other hand, see the turmoil as an opportunity for growth.

Loving relationships can generally stand up to much more unevenness and pressure than you may have given them credit for; in fact, they often thrive on it. As the English poet William Blake noted, "Without contraries is no progression." And progression, rather than some imagined ideal of immutable, frozen loveliness, may be the real secret of successful, healthy relationships.

So if you and your mate have been moving unevenly through the phases of your union, perhaps you should be elated rather than depressed. Lack of conflict may make a relationship arid and keep one or both partners stuck in a particular phase, unable or unwilling to move for fear of upsetting the other. As you'll see many times in this book, such rigidity ensures the escalation of conflict, and eventually can destroy the relationship itself.

Because of the changing nature of relationships, one that is growing and vital requires that each person be a unique, independent individual who contributes to the union by sharing and participating with the other. In the best relationships, being out of phase with your mate will more than likely reflect a healthy sense of autonomy, or a personal integrity distinct from the union, rather than proof of impending disaster.

People who establish successful loving unions do so by letting the other person be a whole person, rather than forcing him or her to be only one-half of a whole. Successful friends, like successful business partners, build on their natural differences to create something more interesting (and more fragile as well, to be sure) than either one of them could have created on his or her own. But they realize that that something must not be allowed to divest either of them of their own unique qualities.

Growth does not occur easily. Growing alongside another distinct human being may be the most difficult kind of growth. For this reason, many relationships cannot survive the push-pull, the shifting polarities, the intermittent discordance, that occurs whenever two people get together. Learning how to love and how to keep your love alive can be done successfully, however, if you first understand the generative power of conflict and then work to develop mechanisms for dealing with it when it arises.

In a three-legged race, the two linked legs function as one while the separate legs remain separate. The couple who wins such a race must be able to coordinate union and independence in much the same way as lovers need to coordinate their dual attractions to separateness and togetherness. To keep your love alive, you and your partner must learn to recognize your simultaneous needs for autonomy and mutuality, as well as the interrelated links between the two. Mutuality prospers and grows when you both function autonomously and enjoy the freedom to be alone—together. At the same time, true freedom often occurs only in a caring, mutually supportive union with another person.

Paradoxically, difficulties in relationships result from an excess of either mutuality or autonomy, while a balanced appreciation of your seemingly self-contradictory needs can enhance both your personal integrity and the strength of the togetherness you share.

Chapter 5

The Fear of Intimacy

Throughout American history, the self-help tradition has emphasized the development of individual gifts and the satisfaction of individual needs. Building from the idea that each person possesses unique qualities, it has stressed the fact that true self-enrichment results from the exploration of the specific desires, fears, and aspirations that differentiate one person from another, not from mutual aid or conformity to a group standard. In recent years, this ethic of self-reliance has reached unfortunately exaggerated proportions in the pop psychology movement. This movement's thrust is that you must "be your own best friend" and "look out for number one."

Now, the emphasis on individual self-enrichment does provide a healthy corrective for the tendency to become too dependent on others. Any philosophy or technique that increases individual autonomy can be beneficial to personal growth, and, being your own person is indeed more enriching than depending on another person's definition. Independence is crucial to relationships, too, since you must have a clear sense of your own separateness to be able to form a productive relationship.

But the search for autonomy can be carried to harmful

extremes. Not every person who sets out to define his or her needs independently does so successfully. Even if you are successful, the excitement of "getting your act together" can be offset by uneasiness and loneliness if you don't have anyone with whom to share the experience. Focusing exclusively on what you personally need to be happy, then, may actually cut you off from certain sources of encouragement—friends, lovers, family—that you need just as much as you need to rely on yourself.

It's easy to cut yourself off from others—at least until the pain of loneliness hits you. You may periodically put up walls between yourself and your loved ones, hoping to avoid the pain you experience when they cannot understand how you feel. Afraid of partial disappointments, you may close yourself off and experience total disappointment. Give and take may seem too difficult or too demeaning; rather than burden yourself with the pressures of human relationships, you may prefer no contact at all.

Such extremes result from an unwillingness to handle the difficult juggling process that is essential to balancing mutuality and autonomy. This process is always difficult, and it can be aggravated by various factors. Physical separation because of the demands of a job, for example, can be such a factor. As much as people want to be independent, being physically apart from their lovers or spouses can be a source of real tension; it can generate feelings of jealousy, insecurity, guilt, and resentment simply as a result of their difficulty in handling separation, not as a result of specific events.

The experience of Philip and Lisa, ostensibly a very independent couple, clearly illustrates this problem.

Jet Nag: Problems of Being Apart

Philip headed the marketing division of a large corporation. His wife, Lisa, worked as a lawyer in a Wall Street law firm. Their work regularly took them in different directions away from their home in New York. Philip might spend two days in Chicago one week while Lisa might be in Baltimore at the beginning of the following week.

You might think that their weekend reunions would be joyous, but just the opposite was the case. Rather than creating pleasant times when they were together, they spent their time in recriminations, protesting how badly they had felt when apart—and blaming each other for the separation. When they came to me for help, it appeared that, in spite of their high degree of individual autonomy, neither one could handle separation well, and that their shared incapacity for confronting the underlying issue had created much tension in their marriage.

In general, people have fewer problems communicating during the approach and mutuality phases of their relationships than they do during the separation phase or afterward when negative feelings from a recently ended separation still remain. Philip and Lisa experienced both these problems of separation. When Lisa left on a business trip, she began to feel guilty knowing Philip would be lonely while she was gone. The same held true when he took his trips. When a trip ended, they would spend hours and sometimes days reflecting bitterly on how uncomfortable they had been—without really confronting why it had made them feel this way. Since they never clarified the issues, the pattern recurred every time one of them took a trip.

Encouraging them to discuss their feelings openly helped to shed some light on their inability to cope with separation. Neither of them, it turned out, had felt secure enough in the relationship to talk about anxieties and fears about the other's independence. This was ironic because independence—that quality of not being "bound" to another—characterized both their respective personalities and in fact had drawn them together in the first place.

Like many couples, Philip and Lisa wanted it both ways. Philip admired Lisa's competent, go-getting personality, and felt proud of her professional achievements. At the same time he resented her independence, since it gave her less time for him. Lisa, on her part, tried to accept Philip's frequent trips, but could not see them as anything other than a personal affront to her. This made her feel resentful, and perpetuated her overall insecurity about the relationship.

Raised in a conventional midwestern family, Lisa feared that she might become, like her mother, a bossy, overprotective hausfrau. It was this fear, in fact, that had motivated her to obtain a law degree, adopt a jet-setting life style, and marry a man who would not want her to sit home with the kids. Her whole life had focused on the attainment of the autonomy her mother lacked. But the attainment of that autonomy, ironically, cut her off from the very man who said he admired it: her independence triggered a defensive independence on his part, which in turn elicited an overprotective bossiness on her part—so that in the end she found herself behaving very much as her mother had behaved.

To be helped this couple had to recognize their strong dependency needs as well as their needs for independence. They had to see how their overly autonomous life styles stifled these needs. Being apart, it turned out, did not prove to be the great delight they had anticipated. What they both had to do was reassess the place of mutuality in their marriage, and make the necessary adjustments in their work schedules to ensure that they could spend more time together.

I pointed out to them that when a couple physically separate and experience discomfort they can make it a valuable mutual experience by discussing their respective feelings. I urged them, therefore, to talk without recrimination and blame: to compare notes, every time they were apart, as to how the experience had made them feel.

Lisa told me this took considerable effort because it meant admitting her own vulnerability. "It's very hard for me to admit how angry and hurt I get, because those are emotions that I think are not very adult or fair. So I try to suppress the fact that I feel that way."

But the suppression did not really work, and Philip saw the resentment all the same. Only when the two of them agreed to acknowledge their mutual interdependence as well as independence did they begin to work things out. Philip observed later in the therapy, "When you think out loud about how you are feeling, that makes a great deal of difference."

Lisa's reluctance to discuss her feelings illustrates a common problem in maintaining a healthy union with a partner: fearful of acknowledging their need for intimacy and their hidden vulnerability, people act as if a brave front will diminish their anxiety, when, ironically, such a front actually increases anxiety and uncertainty about the union. I have seen this in countless sessions with patients. As long as they remain unwilling to acknowledge their vulnerability, it remains a problem. When they can say, "I feel rejected" or "You hurt my feelings," the sense of vulnerability quickly dissolves. Acknowledging pain generally diminishes its importance, while defending against it only increases its severity.

Lisa and Philip's problem was not uncommon. Many people find it difficult to express their feelings. Fearful of hurting and alienating their loved ones, they decide not to talk about the anxieties of separation—or about any other anxieties. This can lead to a pattern of "stonewalling" behavior, in which a series of more or less honest denials takes the place of a real interchange. At its worst this can lead to a total cessation of communication.

Denials: Deciding Not to Talk

A patient of mine named Helen, who felt she was on the verge of divorce, once described with great bitterness her husband Paul's particular brand of stonewalling: according to her, he isolated himself every night, withdrawing from her sexually, watching television instead of communicating. "He just won't talk," she complained.

"He'll sit and he'll listen to me lecture. He doesn't care enough to talk back. I wouldn't take some of the things I do to him. I try to see how far I can push him. So he'll finally talk, and open up, and do me a favor by letting me see how he's feeling. If he really cared about me, he'd do that all the time. He'd tell me, so I could change something, so I could do something differently. Instead he broods. I don't know what he's feeling."

Helen's frustration and resentment, so apparent in her complaint, resulted from her feeling that Paul didn't care enough about her—an accurate interpretation of the hostility implicit in his silence.

In any relationship, *all* forms of behavior, not just verbal ones, have a communicative function. Thus Paul's refusal to communicate, although he proclaimed it was innocuous, and motivated by his desire to avoid a fight, proved to be a very forceful method of communication, compelling Helen to react with vehement frustration and rage.

Silence constitutes an extreme form of stonewalling. Somewhat milder forms can be observed in any relationship in which one party controls the floor and dominates the conversation while the other party talks only reluctantly. The justification for this kind of denial reveals much about both the attractiveness and the inherent dangers of feeling yourself to be apart.

In chapter 3, I discussed one of the most common of these justifications: the "terrible simplifications" of denying that a problem exists. Such a denial effectively closes off communication. Additional common explanations include the convictions that "talking only makes matters worse," that you "just can't put it into words," and that you'd "rather be left alone." Let's look at these forms of denial a little more closely:

1. "Talking makes matters worse." Talking may indeed make some matters worse in the short run, but, by and large, problems do not resolve themselves if you ignore them. Most couples repeat the same arguments and experience the same resentments over and over again. By not confronting the issues that trouble them, they grow further and further apart, the taboo issues increase in number, and they reach a point where they cannot discuss anything at all. In the end, fearful of making problems worse, they leave them unsettled and smouldering.

Moreover, denial invariably leads, as it did in Helen's case, to increased resentment and a kind of nervous, forced separateness that can be an even more painful experience than the issue at hand. In this kind of situation, the way the differences are handled (or rather, *not* handled) becomes even more of a problem than the differences themselves. Discussing the unpleasant, on the other hand, can reinforce healthy autonomy by making you both aware of your differences and of the problems you have yet to resolve.

2. "I don't know how I feel" and "I can't say exactly what I mean" have become quite common convictions in a society in which partners demand of one another "full disclosure" of innermost thoughts. On one hand, the failure to define your feelings can block true communication. On the other hand, the search for the definition often confuses and complicates communication. The tendency to overanalyze, to look for hidden meanings, to dig for symbols and codes, can lead you miles away from the understanding you are trying to grasp.

You may want to avoid dealing with your real feelings —they may embarrass you or make you feel too vulnerable, or cause pain to your partner—and so you bury them in complicated analysis. Feelings of loneliness, jealousy, and shattered self-esteem are often the most difficult to express. It's easier for most people to disguise these feelings as anger or frustration or even physical discomfort.

The only solution is to try to be honest, and try to communicate. Sharing your feelings enhances communication. At first, you may feel awkward and anxious about discussing your feelings, and that's only normal. But with practice and the recognition of the acceptability and naturalness of your "bad" as well as your "good" feelings, you can learn to discuss them.

Say you've just been kept waiting for twenty minutes

while your spouse finishes some shopping that you consider frivolous. It may make you uncomfortable to acknowledge your resentment, but to call it something else,
or to say you can't quite put your finger on how you feel
not only prevents fruitful interaction but also closes off a
window into your own soul. If you do this long enough,
you'll find yourself alienated from everyone, including
yourself. Thus your attempt to keep things running
smoothly can simply create more "counterproductive independence."

3. "Just leave me alone." The ultimate justification for
refusing to communicate stems from the conviction that,
like a hit-and-run lover, you're involved in the relationship only part time, and your real destiny lies somewhere
else, somewhere "out there," alone. This constitutes the
crux of the autonomy-mutuality problem. Many people
delude themselves into thinking that they can maintain a
relationship while remaining fully committed to independence or to romantic loneliness. Like the Greta Garbo
character in *Grand Hotel* (the ballerina who just "wants
to be alone"), or like the wandering gunslinger characters
in countless Westerns, they try to form relationships with
one eye already on the door—and then wonder why the
relationships so abruptly dissolve.

You cannot get something for nothing, you cannot find
love on a hit-and-run basis, you cannot expect to satisfy
your mutuality and your autonomy simultaneously. The
best you can do is to achieve a balance by eliminating the
illusion that communication equals entrapment. If you
cannot do that, you may be able to develop your intellectual or artistic capacity brilliantly, but you will almost
certainly stunt your emotional growth, because emotional
growth depends ultimately on the ways you relate to others.

Those who strive to maintain a loving relationship without expecting to sacrifice some autonomy have little chance of achieving their goal, while those who succeed in keeping their love alive do so by a commitment, paradoxically, to both dependence and independence.

Avoiding Intimacy

In *Games People Play,* the late Eric Berne described the "Frigid Woman" ploy in which a sexually confused wife, seeking proof that she still appeals to her husband, parades before him half-naked until he begins to respond. Then, frightened by her wish come true, she yells, "All men are beasts!," storms away from him, and locks her door.

This not uncommon scenario illustrates a way of relating common to people who both desire and fear physical closeness. They want assurance of their desirability, but cannot acknowledge the psychological dependency on their partners that that assurance would signify. Hungry for affection, they cannot form the intimate bonds of friendship that could make the affection a normal, everyday condition rather than an intermittent (and intermittently frustrated) proof of sexiness. In other words, they want to get only so close and no closer, because while they desire the "strokes" that a romantic partner can give them, they are terribly wary of intimacy per se.

Most people fear real intimacy to some extent, and engage in all kinds of self-protective maneuvers to ensure that they will not get so close to others that they risk being hurt. Developing intimacy almost always activates the anticipation of rejection; for this reason most people rarely give fully of themselves.

Sometimes this happens even to people who appear to

be extremely open to others. A patient of mine named Roberta seemed content with a rather promiscuous life style, although she admitted, "I do hope that some day I'll get together with somebody special, you know? I like the men I go out with, but I can't seem to get really close. I guess that sometimes I miss that."

Her promiscuity, as I explained to her, did not help her to get to know the variety of people that she supposed it would. On the contrary, her casual style functioned as a *distancing factor*, enabling her to substitute fleeting friendships for firm ones, and protecting her from the truly scary prospect of closeness.

"Sometimes," Roberta told me, "you can get very close to people even in a casual relationship. You can talk about surprisingly intimate things with a person you've only just met."

"Sure," I admitted, "that's true. But it's the intimacy of a tavern. You can tell a stranger the most intimate details about yourself because the chances are you'll never see the person again and the psychological risks are small. You're not putting yourself on the line. You're pretending to be close because tomorrow the guy will be gone. It's much harder and much more frightening for you to open up to somebody you have a close relationship with."

"Maybe you're right," she replied. "But I do want a closer relationship too. I guess I prefer to keep a distance most of the time, but I'd like to close the distance with somebody. How do I get over this?"

Roberta had to learn that the autonomy she prized so highly simply could not evolve within the context of an intimate union. No matter how close you may feel to your loved ones, you retain a need for your own separate identity; yet that need must exist side by side with a commitment to mutuality as long as the union exists. Without this commitment, you'll experience little more than serial monogamy, or a pattern of hit-and-run romances like Roberta's. Close unions demand emotional changes from the people involved; entering a close union without being willing to acknowledge mutuality sets the stage for disaster.

Close unions can give you many things you cannot get on your own, including a satisfaction of mutual needs, emotional support, a sharing of dependencies, and an intimacy that no casual union can create. Roberta avoided all of these. She felt that having her dependency needs fulfilled would indicate weakness and a loss of independence on her part. Afraid that a man would take control of her and be too demanding, she held on tightly to her autonomy and approached relationships casually; this led to repeated disappointments. Reluctant to acknowledge her own dependency needs, she ended up expressing these needs in feelings of loneliness and rage at being treated casually herself. Therapy focused on helping her understand that she could express dependency needs without losing her independence and could *share* in a relationship.

Some women sometimes experience a more extreme fear of intimacy, which is expressed in terms of a fantasied fear that if they allow a man into their psychological space, they will relinquish all control over their own lives and put themselves at the mercy of the man's whims. Such women may even avoid all contact with men, especially those they find attractive, isolating themselves behind a psychological wall and allowing no one to enter or touch them.

This syndrome occurs all too often in our culture. So

fervently do people pursue individuality that they often believe that entering a close union will mean the loss of self. They fear being swallowed up by the union, and becoming merely a "better half" (or a worse half) to their partners. The sense of fusion that frequently accompanies the approach phase of a relationship convinces them that if they continue drawing close they will fuse forever with the other person, and thus sacrifice themselves to the union.

This is an unnecessary worry. While the approach phase can temporarily obliterate feelings of distinction between lovers, your own natural sense of self will ultimately step in to right the balance and ensure that your autonomy will be preserved. You simply cannot be swallowed up by another person as long as you remain aware of your need for union and your need for separateness. The fear of engulfment by another constitutes a chimera that makes it easier to maintain distance between yourself and others.

This is especially true of people who fear closeness because they feel themselves unworthy of love. In such instances the acknowledged fear of entrapment serves as a disguise for the actual fear that the lover will seduce and abandon you—treating you, in short, in the demeaning way you "deserve." Again this relates to the common human fear that love sets you up for rejection.

Roberta's problem shows how the fear of rejection can be translated into social activity that seems to indicate just the opposite of that fear. Clearly, women do not have a monopoly on such fears. In our culture, in fact, the fear of intimacy appears more frequently as a masculine characteristic, part of the still powerful machismo that demands of any "real" man a stolid indifference to turmoil and a sphinx-like commitment to silence. Indeed, the avoidance of intimacy may be the linchpin of the current masculine ideal.

The Tragicomedy of Isolation

At the end of the popular Western *Shane*, Alan Ladd, having foiled the bad guys, rides off into the sunset to the echoing sounds of a young boy's desperate pleas: "Shane! Shane! Come back, Shane!" But of course Shane does not come back. He has finished his work in this place. He has other wrongs to right, and nothing remains to keep him here. So he returns to what he knows best, the wanderer's way: a life of constant motion and repressed emotion.

The strong, silent ways of countless Shanes have been presented to generations of film fans as noble and ultimately manly. In terms of the subject of this book, their stories converge on one abiding notion: the hero, the real man, the good guy, cannot have very much to do with human relationships. The hero must not only be fast on the draw, he must be unattached. By definition, Western heroes, like private eyes, function alone. Their lives on the open range or in the concrete jungles symbolize a kind of mythical noncontingent and pseudoindependent autonomy that appeals, commonly and predictably, to boys in their teens who see the prospect of jobs, family, and home looming in the distance, and who would prefer to remain boys forever.

Both the myth of the Western hero and the Hollywood/Harlequin image of romance reflect the difficulty inherent in finding real intimacy in twentieth-century America. The Western film's notion of the ideal male hero as a man without a home, without a job, most of all without a romantic partner, no doubt suggests the tremendous ambivalence that many men feel about relating to women, and provides a fantasy that temporarily enables them to feel comfortable about their failure to do so. The sissy or the shopkeeper sits home at night with the little woman. The real man, the model the viewer can easily identify with, barely speaks to women at all, takes on no responsibility for interacting with them, and views the idea of settling down as an infringement on his freedom. At the end of the movie Shane rides off while the boy's father resumes his woodcutting. It's obvious the boy wants to go with Shane, but he cannot. He could not fit in with Shane's life, for Shane's self-imposed destiny is to avoid entanglements, responsibilities, and love.

The untrammeled, semi-mute hero has been a dominant figure in our popular mythology throughout this century—from William S. Hart through Gary Cooper and Marlon Brando to Clint Eastwood. His attraction lies at least partly in the fullness of his dedication to the ideal of autonomy as opposed to the more complicated real-life task of forging an ongoing love based on autonomy and mutuality.

It takes hard work to form enduring close attachments and to transform infatuation into intimacy. No wonder, then, that Hollywood fantasies ennoble silence and turn weakness into strength, substituting a spectrum of meaningful glances for communication.

In recent years the inexpressive male has diminished a little in popularity, as people have become more comfortable with expressing their feelings. The strong, silent image, however, still remains—reflecting the persistence of communication problems.

Ironically, according to the myth, those long silences

reflect a deep, almost unfathomable sensitivity, not evidence of stupidity or orneriness. This makes them difficult to condemn. When Marlon Brando grunts a monosyllable, he conveys the notion that only the torment of his complex soul makes it impossible for him to express the rich emotional understanding behind it. This attractive idea appeals to plenty of men, from eighteen to eighty, who willingly emulate it, since it saves them from the embarrassment of intimacy.

Nobody can say for certain whether those unplumbed depths really are profound, or just empty, but in terms of interactional response, it really makes very little difference. As you've seen in the case of Paul and Helen, a partner often perceives unspoken emotion as indistinguishable from apathy. Marlon Brando may be able to pull this kind of thing off, but for most people silence remains a losing game—one that may, quite unjustly, lead your partners to judge you more harshly than you deserve. As someone I know once observed about a strong, silent man who had taken her to dinner, "It took me three hours to get him to talk, and when he did, you know what I started to think? This guy's just as dumb as he acts."

Tragically, in his zeal to remain aloof from sticky entanglements, the independent hero cuts himself off from a range of communication that could actually enhance rather than limit his chance for happiness. Fearful of ever surrendering himself to another person because that other person might betray or harm him, he never discovers that everybody else, just like him, experiences fear, loneliness, and a feeling of vulnerability. No one can be certain about his or her worthiness to be loved; everyone becomes tongue-tied when it comes to acknowledging the urge toward union. The Western hero may be a pathological example of the human inability to relate openly to others, but his isolation represents the experience of many, not a few.

Most of you don't allow fear to overcome you to the point that you physically isolate yourselves from the rest of humanity for long stretches of time, but in a way what you do may be worse: you stay in close contact with others, and reconcile yourselves to anxiety. The real tragi-comedy of this whole business is that when you do attempt to reach out to another person, you often find that the other person has been trying to reach out to you for a long time. Recognition of this common human dilemma can be a frustrating but also liberating experience. The astonishing discovery of union is that striving for intimacy can make you not more but actually less vulnerable.

Considering how obstructive of communication, how damaging to intimacy, the dedication to independence without mutuality can be, it's not surprising that many spouses, confronted with silence or muddy expression, strive desperately to get their partners to relate to them, or that they work overtime to offset the pull of autonomy and put mutuality to the fore. Faced with a brooding, uncommunicative partner, it seems evident to many people that only "harder work" will make the relationship prosper. Despite the logic of this you should realize that sometimes a full-fledged dedication to union can be every bit as damaging as a full-fledged dedication to oneself. It's the problems associated with too much mutuality, therefore, that I want to consider now.

Chapter 6

Separation Anxiety

Few emotions are as uncomfortable and potentially debilitating to human beings as the fear of being left alone. This fear causes couples to stay together in many long-term relationships even when real intimacy is absent. While people fear intimacy, they fear separation even more, and often see it as a sign of imminent disaster even when they cannot tolerate togetherness or are drawn to other relationships.

Separation anxiety, or the anxiety associated with separation from a loved one, is the obverse of the fear of intimacy that we discussed in the last chapter. As we will see in this chapter, it can be just as problematic as its opposite.

Most people are uncomfortable both in being alone and in being too close to others; they often view romance as the ultimate resolution of this dilemma, since it eliminates solitude and produces a heightened sense of oneness with the loved person. This sense of oneness has characteristics of euphoria, a special state in which intimacy is experienced without self-consciousness. Unfortunately, this heightened state seldom lasts long, and as a result the most united lovers inevitably experience the sense of separateness that is so often a source of problems. This is especially true when a mate is viewed as the "other half" or the "better self," not as a distinct, autonomous individual.

Earlier I cited a passage from Barbara Cartland's *The Dangerous Dandy,* in which the hero and heroine come together in an embrace that makes them "no longer two but one." Here love (and sex) dissolves duality and overcomes separateness by fusing the lovers into a union that has an integrity and permanence lacking in each of them as individuals. Most lovers would agree that romantic union creates a kind of ultimate fusion with a transcendent quality of its own, but when the relationship thus supersedes the needs of the people in it—when one or both partners attempt to perpetuate this transcendental state without realizing that it developed when two separate people came together—problems inevitably occur.

In fact, intense feelings of intimacy actually require separation. Separation is necessary not only for the growth of the separate autonomous lives of the two people in a relationship, but also for making possible the intensity of the relationship itself. I have seen many married couples live in conflict with each other out of a sense of obligation to the relationship; they were continually resentful of their very intimacy because it was coupled with a denial of self-interest and a failure to accept their individual needs.

People who are committed out of a sense of loyalty, tradition, or family pressure to honor the demands of the relationship at all costs generally adopt elaborate explanations to convince themselves that their commitment makes sense. Because of the fear of separation, and because of the fear of marital failure that might follow, many people involved in satisfactory but conflict-ridden relationships are reluctant to acknowledge the existence of problems. When friction surfaces, they become fearful and make every effort to deny or minimize the problem rather than try to resolve their difficulties.

A case in point is the marriage of Bill and Kathy. College sweethearts, they married early—before either of them had reached a satisfactory level of individual independence. Their subsequent relationship was characterized by too great a tendency to project their own faults on to each other, and by a constant mutual restriction of each other's movements, activity, and spontaneity. Togetherness had become a straitjacket for both of them; it kept them in constant warfare with each other until they sought help.

Treatment focused on helping them develop new ways of interacting so as to be able to tolerate their differences and learn to express their unique independent characteristics. They learned to listen to each other and to respond nondefensively. As a result of this they became more appreciative of each other and began to relate more as genuine friends than in terms of the fixed and repetitive roles of husband and wife.

Pseudomutuality

In many relationships the avoidance of separation becomes such a dominant pattern that a forced, tense mutuality takes the place of real affection. The couple do everything together not out of desire but out of the fear of being alone and thereby jeopardizing the relationship. Psychologist Israel Charney has described this situation as follows:

[Many] a couple unconsciously work together to sweep under the rug their various disagreements and antagonisms so as to dovetail with each other in a seemingly smooth-flowing way that wipes out the experiencing of problems and, more importantly, the experiencing of separate individuality.*

This relationship Charney calls *pseudomutuality,*

In their provocative book *Change,* Stanford researchers Paul Watzlawick, John Weakland, and Richard Fisch pointed to the fundamental similarity between two self-destructive forms of pseudomutuality. "Both the simplifier and the utopian," they write, "strive for a problemless world—the one by denying that certain difficulties exist at all, the other by acknowledging their existence but defining them as basically abnormal and therefore capable of resolution."† These two responses to difficulties commonly occur in relationships characterized by an emphasis on mutuality, where one or both parties pay excessive attention to the demands or needs of the relationship often at the expense of individual needs. Faced with crippling interactional problems, they either deny those problems or insist that they can be worked out simply by the "power of love."

Just as terrible simplification can actually intensify rather than alleviate problems, so too can utopian solutions complicate interpersonal difficulties—when, for example, one partner insists that love eventually (and always) triumphs over misunderstanding. When lovers view "being in love" as an ultimate goal of human existence and are "in love *with* love," there is considerable opportunity for the distortion of affection.

*Israel Charney, *Marital Love and Hate* (New York: Macmillan, 1972), pp. 36–37.
†Watzlawick et al., *Change* (New York: Norton, 1974), p. 47n.

The parties involved in what I earlier called "Love with a capital L" seem like acolytes at a shrine, especially when their denial of difficulties accompanies a commitment to pseudomutuality. The problem with this is that interpersonal love is a very different emotion—as well it ought to be—from worship.

Right Little, Tight Little Islands

In the days before naval imperialism dragged them kicking into a global world, British isolationists used to speak of their country as a "right little, tight little island," the implication being that no problems existed at home and that contact with other people and other ways of life could only undermine the national integrity. Many couples adopt a similar attitude, insisting that their right little, tight little unions, in order to survive, must avoid contact with the outside world. Fearful of contamination, they isolate themselves in "love nests" and look balefully at the external world, a world that can never be privy to their special bliss.

The poets have, of course, praised this kind of relationship for centuries. Some of the world's most famous romantic lyrics celebrate unions built on the premise of a dangerous world and the safety of retreat. Recall, for example, Matthew Arnold's poignant pleas, uttered on the sands of Dover Beach:

> Ah, love, let us be true
> To one another! for the world, which seems
> To lie before us like a land of dreams,
> So various, so beautiful, so new,
> Hath really neither joy, nor love, nor light,
> Nor certitude, nor peace, nor help for pain.

Or think of Romeo and Juliet, probably the most famous lovers in literature. "Star-crossed" and committed absolutely to each other, they commit suicide rather than live in a world in which they cannot be together. Their tragic ending has always been seen as a noble act, but it really should be seen as an exaggerated form of passive or dependent loving. However moving Shakespeare's poetry may be, the play still suggests that his two lovers cannot survive on their own. Unable to be autonomous, they commit themselves to a permanent though lifeless mutuality.

Another example of the destructiveness inherent in solutions to separation anxiety can be found in the pathological patterns of people who kill their husbands or wives. Spouse murderers commonly have elaborate fantasy images of love, and react violently when these images prove unrealistic. In one study, Drs. George and Roger Bach found that resentment at having a "perfect" union go bad often motivated the murderer:

> The killings involved the motivation to punish a partner for not fitting into a role, image, or situation as defined and wished for by the other. Spouse killers experienced their spouses as "spoilers" of what they had wishfully fantasized would make the relationship fulfilling. This fantasy expectation tended to follow the romantic model of love.*

Seeing the world as threatening, then, can be simply a way of denying autonomy and reinforcing pseudomutuality. In a noted study of the "Romeo and Juliet effect," Richard Driscoll and his associates demonstrated that this does not in fact make for healthy, productive unions. In-

*Cited in George Bach and Herb Goldberg, *Creative Aggression* (New York: Doubleday, 1974), p. 64.

vestigating the relationship between romantic love and parental or other external resistance, they found that external threats to "love nest" types of relationships originally intensified the lovers' fondness for each other, but that this intensification of feelings led ultimately to interpersonal tension, and in many cases to the later breakup of the unions.* Hardening the line against the outside, then, led to precisely the opposite effect from the one the lovers intended: coming closer together for mutual support eventually contributed to their coming apart.

This paradox indicates again that in any viable union there must be a balance between "twoness" and "oneness," between shared, mutual interests and the individual needs of both parties to be alone and separate. With a denial of either autonomy or mutuality, the union cannot last long. An excessive dedication to autonomy leads to sterile, stonewalling tactics, and an excessive dedication to "the two of us" leads to pseudomutuality. Repression of autonomy leads to resentment in at least one and probably in both parties, and when resentment grows, no "Heaven-sent" devotion on earth can overcome its corrosive effects.

This suggests how damaging the "love nest" syndrome can be—and how in an attempt to eliminate separation anxiety, couples very often bring about a result opposite to the one they were hoping for. Afraid of being left alone, they cling to a false closeness, a false security, until that very closeness becomes distasteful to them—and they end up running from each other in disgust, having elicited exactly the reaction they had hoped to avoid. This is the

*Richard Driscoll, Keith Davis, and Milton Lipetz, "Parental Influence and Romantic Love: the Romeo and Juliet Effect" in *Journal of Personality and Social Psychology* 24, no. 1 (1972).

unpleasant paradox of pseudomutuality: you often produce the results you fear by trying too hard.

Isolation didn't work for the British, and it doesn't work
for couples either. As John Donne said, "No man is an
island"; that holds true for couples as well as individuals.
Unless you live in the wilderness, it's virtually impossible
to keep your distance entirely from other people. In fact,
the more fervently couples proclaim their isolation, the
more likely they will end up inviting the very pressures
they try to avoid and the threatening contacts they fear
will disrupt them.

Thus couples who insist on dealing only with each
other, on throwing up a common bulwark against the
world, usually experience trouble. A natural, flowing
movement between your spouse and other people, in
other words, should be a lot easier to handle in the long
run than an artificially constrained and isolated "love
unit."

Now, not all dependent partners spend their time gazing into each other's eyes and trying to forget about the
world. Pseudomutuality comes in other forms as well.

Patterns of Poor Mutuality

Many relationships involve an ostensibly dominant
partner and an ostensibly submissive partner who depends on the dominant one to take care of him or her. In
most unions, though, whatever the appearances, both
partners actually depend on each other. One common
pattern is that of *complementary dependence,* in which
each partner acts reciprocally toward the other: when
one criticizes, the other apologizes, always balancing one

behavior with its opposite. Another pattern is *symmetrical dependence,* in which one partner mirrors the behavior of the other in a well-balanced and highly synchronized fashion, each partner taking turns in acting the same way toward the other. Thus, if you criticize your partner, he will criticize you; if you apologize, he will apologize, and so on.

Those are common overall patterns. The specific modes in which they make their appearances can vary greatly. Consider the following examples:

1. Dependence on Dependency

Julius Fast, in his popular book *Body Language,* describes a pathological pattern of interaction between a "submissive" wife and a "dominant" husband. Every night upon returning from work, the husband, Ralph, puts his wife, Annie, through the same agony of wondering whether he finds the dinner acceptable. He eats in stony silence while she waits passively for his verdict. When he finally deigns to nod approval, the tension abruptly breaks, "Life is wonderful, and Ralph is her love, and she is terribly, terribly happy." The dinnertime soap opera seems cruel and pointless, but as Fast notes, "The question of whether Annie is a victim or an accomplice is not for us to decide. . . . The sado-masochistic relationship benefits both of them in a strange way."*

Numerous couples relate in the same way, with the husband and wife depending on each other's dependency and providing each other with a support they cannot pro-

*Julius Fast, *Body Language* (New York: Pocket Books, 1971), pp. 61–63.

vide for themselves. That is to say, they have great difficulty satisfying their own dependency needs, but do so indirectly by maintaining control over each other. It is important to note that Ralph is as dependent here as Annie—although he seems to be "in control." This is true of many "take charge" people.

In fact, people who must constantly take control actually have an inordinate need to seek approval, though they may lack the skills or inclination to seek this directly. Business and political leaders who surround themselves with yes men exhibit this need to a marked degree. So do those spouses, like Ralph, who transform bossiness and being "one up" on their partners into a predictable daily pattern.

In effect the need to control can be just as much a manifestation of dependency as the need to obey. This pattern commonly occurs in relationships in which neither party has the maturity to allow and encourage growth in the other. If two such people marry early, they may be subsidized by parents who remain overinvolved in their lives, and keep them bound in a perpetual dependency. One wife I know acted helplessly dependent while manipulating her husband into feeling guilty for the inequality in their relationship. Inclined to dominate and control her anyway, he masked his own dependency on the situation by behaving in a superficially authoritarian manner. Like Ralph, he insisted that dinner be on the table at the same time each day, and in many other little ways as well he endeavored to keep it clear who was boss.

This couple had to learn how complementary patterns of relating stifled their own individual needs, since they established a routine way of relating that precluded change and established a false sense of security and stabil-

ity. This made it difficult to change or shift without causing considerable anxiety and uncertainty.

2. Talking It to Death

Gene and Tammy seemed to be in an interminable
discussion about their relationship. They had pledged to
be open with each other, and to that end they made every
minor disagreement, every small tension between them,
an opportunity to completely re-evaluate their togetherness. They saw nothing as passing or insignificant; everything had significance as an omen or a sign. Not surprisingly, this intense dedication to talking things out
eventually got out of hand, and they found themselves
unable to discuss anything *but* the relationship. This wore
them down. Seeing everything through a supposed "mutual lens" led to overexamination and resentment; within
a couple of months, their commitment to full disclosure
had backfired. They became bored with the ongoing analysis and split up, recognizing dimly that they had talked
the relationship to death.

The partners in relationships should know when to talk
and when to keep quiet. Gene and Tammy could not
draw that distinction, because like many modern couples
they viewed openness as a virtue and silence as secrecy.
In their zeal to get things clear, they only made matters
worse. They lost sight of common interests and ended up
analyzing each other's motives and bringing about the
unfortunate results they had tried to avoid.

Knowing when to talk and when to keep quiet can be
difficult to determine. You are always communicating.
The important thing to learn is that you communicate not
merely by words but also by tones, gestures, and body

language—often without being aware of it. The best communication may be when you are talking about your own feelings and not attacking your partner. When you are clear about the message you are conveying and are not trying to order your spouse around, you communicate better than when you put your partner on the defensive. You can find out whether you are getting your message across by checking with your partner, clarifying your messages to make certain he or she heard what you said and took it as you meant it. People cannot do this if you attack them and put them on the defensive.

An essential part of healthy mutuality involves a discussion of difficulties. But a constant emphasis on mutuality itself can become counterproductive, since it creates anxiety and uncertainty and may initiate a vicious circle of unending defensiveness rather than a resolution of differences or a mutual acceptance of uncertainty.

Most relationships need a certain level of ambiguity, of unstated opinions, of silence. An obsession with talking things over, no less than a need to be constantly together, generally reflects poor mutuality rather than real affection. Carried to an extreme, as in Gene and Tammy's case, it can hasten a decline.

3. "What Do You Think About It, Dear?"

The need to solicit your partner's opinion on every single issue of common interest may occur together with an inability to remain silent and may appear mistakenly as an example of sharing. People who need to know what their spouse thinks in every situation before making a decision betray their own inability to make autonomous decisions. The conviction that a shared decision, which takes account of both parties' input, is better than a unilateral decision is based usually on one or both partners' inability to trust his own judgment.

Past experiences, not the facts at hand, govern most opinions. Asking your spouse to decide things for you, therefore, can be evidence that you mistrust your own past decisions, and want him or her to correct your bad thinking in the future. Letting another person take over your responsibility like this reflects dependency—no matter how much the other person loves you.

Some decisions, naturally, require mutual discussion. Any decision that seriously affects both partners should be discussed by both partners. You wouldn't buy a new house or a new car without discussing it with your spouse. You wouldn't plan a vacation or your child's schooling on your own. Working out decisions like this should be characterized by a weighing of equally valid judgments as to how something ought to be done. But if it becomes a matter of checking every decision with your partner, you have moved beyond mutual decision making into a realm of interdependent helplessness.

Healthy mutuality, then, requires independent thinking. The fewer opinions you seek, the more independent you will become. And the more independent you be-: come, the more satisfactory your relationship will be.

4. The Martyr Role

The martyr role is a highly dependent one. It differs from the dependent-on-dependency role inasmuch as it is played by individuals, not couples.

Self-sacrifice, even though it may appear exemplary on the surface, induces guilt in others, limits their sense of freedom, and may even destroy a relationship. Dependency, jealousy, and fear of abandonment all inhibit genuine relationships. Disguised in the form of greater concern for pleasing your partner than for pleasing yourself, self-sacrifice may backfire, and your partner may grow uncertain about you and guilty about your "goodness."

Self-imposed martyrdom becomes a problem when people have to decide what to share and how to share. There is no doubt that sharing can help you and your partner get closer if you choose activities that you both enjoy. But you want to avoid the trap of doing what you don't want half the time and letting your partner do what he or she wants to do the rest of the time.

In *Active Loving*, I described the "fifty-fifty trap" of constant compromise, of constant "going along," in which in an effort to share, couples agree to trade off unwelcome responsibilities on an equal-time basis. Such a system seldom works effectively, since it makes both partners unwilling martyrs. Instead of feeling relieved of half your problems, you both feel distressed all the time. The fifty-fifty trap can lead you to "feeling resentful about doing what you don't want to do 50 percent of the time and to feeling guilty about imposing on others the other 50 percent of the time."* This pattern occurs frequently in relationships characterized by excessive mutuality.

5. "I'm Sorry (You Bastard)"

Conventional wisdom states that the honest admission of faults helps to clear troubled waters and get things started on a clean slate again. Sadly, this does not always

*Ari Kiev, *Active Loving* (New York: Crowell, 1979), pp. 23–24.

work out in practice. Very often, apology can be used as a way not of settling matters but of controlling the person to whom you apologize. You may feel truly sorry for the wrongs you have committed, but if you constantly present *mea culpas* to your partner, he or she may be more resentful than mollified. Being the recipient of constant apologies makes a person feel he may have misjudged you in the first place. "If she's so nice as to apologize," he thinks, "maybe she wasn't wrong after all. Maybe I was wrong." And he immediately starts feeling guilty.

When you assume responsibility for someone else's distress, your good intentions usually backfire, particularly if the other person feels indebted to you for your "kindness." This pattern may even escalate into accusations and indictments. By pretending to be responsible for a partner's problems, you may find your partner gradually believing that you *have* caused his or her distress. Insincere apologies—apologies made to dismiss the subject rather than to resolve the question—can aggravate a troubled relationship as well. Of course insincerity at any time —no matter how well intentioned—is a dangerous or foolish gamble.

Be careful of good intentions. As Thoreau once observed of an inveterate do-gooder, "When I see somebody coming to do me a favor, I run as fast as I can the other way." Nobody likes to be indebted to another person, and constant apology as a way of maintaining mutual peace can do exactly the same thing to your partner as the do-gooder did to Thoreau: make him or her feel timid and worried. You may think you're doing your partner a favor by admitting your guilt: actually you may just be transferring that guilt on to him.

Benjamin Franklin called attention to this curious fact

in an illuminating observation. If he wanted to get on someone's good side, he said, he allowed that person to do him a small favor. That permitted the person to feel that Franklin was in *his* debt, and he became, ironically, much more inclined to help him out again in the future than he would have been if Franklin had done him the favor. Obviously Franklin's expertise extended beyond the political.

Now, all the behaviors I've been describing—complementary and symmetrical patterns of relating, excessive analysis of the relationship, reliance on others' advice, self-sacrifice, and apology—reflect relationships with a bad balance between mutuality and autonomy, relationships in which the partners are suspicious of autonomy and fearful of separation, and where they overemphasize the value of mutuality. These behavioral patterns stem in large part from the fact that for most couples anything seems preferable to being alone.

Nevertheless, being alone can enhance togetherness as well as individuality. The best, most loving, most productive relationships go through periods of separation. Those that survive this necessary phase of close unions grow during separation rather than retreat from it.

Growth from Separation

Separation, whether by choice or circumstances, can be valuable in the development both of your own autonomy and of your relationship. Separation provides an opportunity to develop certain psychological skills for coping with a wide range of emotional reactions to a powerful experience. The following are some of those skills.

1. *Riding out feelings.* Probably the most important coping skills to develop are those that will help you in the reduction of distressing emotions. Finding yourself alone when you are accustomed to being together can lead to depression, jealousy, anxiety, panic, or a sense of imminent doom. Some people become intensely jealous and begin making efforts to keep track of their partners. Others seek out the company of friends or companions and become involved in conflicting loyalties.

These are understandable but counterproductive reactions. The best course of action to follow during a separation is to focus your efforts on becoming familiar with the uncomfortable feelings rather than rush to eliminate them by trying desperately to change the external circumstances that may seem to be the cause of your distress. One technique is to *time* an uncomfortable feeling and determine its duration, associated thoughts, thoughts that intensify the distress, and thoughts or activities that reduce it. In this way you can become familiar with the natural history of the emotion as you experience it and thus can be better prepared to cope with it when it appears again.

Timing the duration of feelings makes them more tolerable. You can do this more readily if you keep in mind the transient nature of negative feelings. Depression, jealousy, anxiety, and loneliness, like all human emotions, pass in time. You can learn to ride them out more easily if you understand that first.

2. *Developing your own interests.* Separation can be especially devastating if you have not developed any interests outside the relationship that contribute to your sense of well-being. If you now find yourself apart, you have a perfect opportunity to renew interests that you

may have enjoyed alone prior to the relationship.

It's not uncommon, especially in close relationships, for couples to feel that they cannot do anything alone: that sports, politics, recreation, everything has to be done together. Because of this, recently separated couples often find themselves with "nothing to do."

I can't tell you what kind of interests will best enrich your nature, but I do know that some individual activity, something you do *only for yourself,* can help you over the distress of separation—and can prepare you for getting back together. As you take up a new language, or start a dahlia garden, you will be re-creating yourself in a richer and more productive mode, and this will add to the richness of the relationship.

I am not suggesting that you abandon everything that gave you and your partner pleasure, only that you expand upon it. Add to your personal repertoire some activity that does not depend on your partner, so that you will not be so overwhelmed by separation when it occurs.

3. *Letting your partner grow.* At the same time, encourage your partner to do the same with his or her interests so that you can grow together without stifling each other with dependency.

This is especially important if you are jealous and possessive. Trying to control your partner often intensifies jealousy and makes you less centered than you would be if you learned to ride out the feelings. Moreover, such negative thinking may set in motion a self-fulfilling prophecy whereby you may bring about the loss of love that you fear. By contrast, you will not lose the relationship if you give it room, but will be strengthening your own sense of self as well as the relationship. The richer your partner becomes, the better it is for you both.

4. *Learning to talk again.* A period of separation some-times can evoke tremendous feelings of resentment and bitterness in both parties, which may explode openly in conflict or may be manifested more subtly by withdrawal. By discussing your feelings honestly and without rancor you can achieve a balanced mutuality. This means being willing to be open about *all* your feelings, not simply expressions of hostility, and being willing to listen and understand your partner's feelings as well.

Separation, then, can be an opportunity to grow and widen your own horizons—both mutually and individu-ally. This, sadly, is lost on many couples, because of the fear of being alone.

Many people unfortunately resist growth, preferring to stay with the familiar rather than ride through the rough terrain of a developing relationship. They make every effort they can to make relationships fit a preordained mold, one that cannot suffer change. The classic Greek tale of the robber Procrustes illustrates by analogy the damage that this does.

Procrustes and the Perfect Fit

In Greek mythology, Procrustes waylaid travelers and forced them to lie down on an iron bed. He stretched those who were too short for the bed until they fit, and chopped off the legs of those who were too tall. Naturally his name has come down to us as a paradigm of inflexibil-ity.

Unfortunately, many people in relationships, con-vinced that a good union must fulfill certain criteria, per-form much the same kind of surgery on themselves, with results almost as dire. Real interpersonal growth means letting the other person be himself or herself with dignity and respect. But many couples fail to realize this: viewing their oneness as the most important thing in the world, they stretch and chop their own beings into impossible configurations, striving for the perfect fit in their own particular iron beds. In the process they succeed not only in restricting each other, but often in killing the relationship as well.

Too few people allow their romantic unions to flow naturally from autonomy to mutuality and back again. Wanting so badly to have them "work" they create a forced mutuality at the expense of differentness and run the risk of creating an explosion or even a dissolution of the relationship. Firming up or stabilizing a relationship almost always inhibits its progression. The minute that you try to create "acceptable" feelings and block out others, you lose the chance of discovering that you can be accepted by another person *just the way you are,* with your faults as well as your virtues. You lose out on discovering that conflict and discontent can be a regenerative rather than damaging force. You lose out on realizing that often it's the attempt to force things into a preconceived shape, like Procrustes did, that leads to the most resentment and pain.

It's easy to miss seeing these things. For example, a compliant spouse may go along willingly with his or her partner's need to romanticize everything. As the idealistic partner becomes increasingly blind to reality, the compliant one may begin to nourish a secret resentment because of the denial of his or her autonomy. The passive, compliant partner, unwilling or unable to express negative emotions about the union, holds them in until the idealizing partner picks up on them and demands more sincerity. This only causes the blocked person to clam up all the more, until resentment and guilt build up so much that all communication is dead.

In effect, the need to perfect the relationship, and not the relationship's inherent imperfections, generally leads to major misunderstandings. As Watzlawick has noted, "The cure is not simply worse than the disease, but rather *is* the disease."* The observation has obvious relevance to the attitude that demands "perfect fits."

Now, poor mutuality results not only from factors within the relationship, but also from patterns learned early in childhood. Passive compliance and excessive devotion to mutuality, whether they lead to a long-term pathological interaction or simply a short-lived union of friction, generally are the result of a compulsive need to reproduce in the present familiar, though uncomfortable, patterns of the past. Understanding the connection between the past and the present, therefore, can help explain why some relationships work so well and why others do not. We'll go into this in the next chapter.

*Watzlawick et al., *Change*, p. 57.

Chapter 7

The Circle Game

Douglaston, a small, sleepy town near the capital of a southern American state, had been settled in the nineteenth century by impoverished Irish farmers. The first generation of workers, fresh from the barren farms of the old country, believed that here in America industriousness would lead automatically to comfort: if they scrimped and saved for the future, they could make more comfortable lives for their children than they had known in Europe.

Unfortunately, their dreams did not materialize. Their children, and eventually their children's children, ended up working in the same mills as their parents, and dreaming the same dream that one day the new generation would break free. Virtually all the townspeople, year after year, followed in their parents' footsteps, every one believing that, next year, things would be different.

For a very few, things did change. Susan Anderson, a friend of mine, was one of these. She told me, with a mixture of bitterness and pride, about breaking free from Douglaston:

"Every girl in that town thinks she's going to be different. You grow up in a family of six kids, seeing both your mama and papa work in the mills, and seeing how your mama can hardly lift her head up she's so tired, and you decide when you reach fifteen or sixteen that this will not happen to you. You're going to get out of it, out of the mills, out of town; you're not going to be tied down to any six kids.

"But then you meet Johnny, and he looks like your passport out. He's young and strong and he wants you, so you say to yourself, sure, I'll marry him and he'll take me away from all this. And you marry him, mostly to get out of the house, and in two years you have two crying kids of your own, and you're living in an even smaller house, and Johnny is working at the mills and you're as tired as your mama ever was. Only now you're the mama, and pretty soon your kids are looking at you and thinking to themselves, I ain't going to end up like her. It goes on like that, mother to daughter, father to son, in a circle."

"How did you break free?" I asked her.

She shook her head in grim memory. "I just picked up and said good-bye. I was seventeen, and scared to death. But I knew what was going to happen to me if I stayed. So I got on a bus for the city, and I went hungry some, and shivered, and cried myself to sleep for a month. But I was free, and that was all that mattered. My girl friends were more scared than I was, and that's why they're still back home. Safe and sound. What they have, see, is something that they know about. It might not be fun, but it's familiar. They'll live it out that way until they die."

It might not be fun, but it's familiar. Susan's words identified for me not only the peculiar miseries of her townspeople's lives, but also a very important principle of human behavior. Despite her fear, she generated enough courage to face the unknown and strike out on her own.

For most of her friends—and for most people, anywhere —the known, the familiar, no matter how unpleasant, remains preferable to the unknown. Like Hamlet, most people would "rather bear those ills we have than fly to others that we know not of." Few people reach for the stars or try something new and unfamiliar; the prospect of striking out into unknown territory disturbs most people sufficiently that they spend their entire lives walking in circles, repeating familiar patterns, rather than taking that first new and unfamiliar step.

This holds true for relationships as well. For most people the patterns established in early childhood, no matter how unsatisfying or frustrating, remain the governing models for all their future behavior. They may seek to define themselves as individuals, to forge unique personal relationships, but in nine cases out of ten, they succeed only in mimicking the less than perfect relationships of their parents and other family members. The victims, not the masters of their destinies, they are doomed to repeat old errors, unable to break free of the known.

Most relationships are governed by automatic behaviors that persist into the present long after they have stopped serving adaptive purposes. Nearly always, these patterns inhibit the development of flexible and growth-producing behavior. We'll examine some of them in this chapter.

Repetitive Patterns

Barbara, an attractive, lively stewardess, regularly experienced difficulty in sustaining close unions. Whenever she became involved in an intimate relationship with a man, she would begin to antagonize him in small ways—

The Circle Game / 119

by breaking dates at the last minute, or criticizing his choice of clothes—until she elicited an angry, defensive response. "It's like I'm only content with a man," she acknowledged with some dismay, "when he's yelling at me."

On the surface Barbara appeared to understand how she was setting herself up for rejection. Yet while she seemed to know what she was doing, she had little control over her behavior.

In most respects, Barbara was an extremely energetic, thoughtful, and self-respecting person; she rarely acted in self-defeating ways. However, when she became too involved with a man, her masochistic tendencies came to the fore, and she began to elicit rejection.

Therapy provided an explanation for this. When she was a child, there were periodic outbursts of temper in her home. Her father, normally gruff, reticent, and preoccupied with his work, had difficulty expressing affection for her and often transferred his frustrations onto Barbara and her mother. While he did not act tyrannical or in a physically abusive way, Barbara grew up believing that only when she had done something wrong could she get his full attention and make real contact with him. At these times his customary silence would vanish and he would criticize her in unmistakable tones.

Eventually Barbara learned to provoke these outbreaks. To her they were evidence of her father's concern, his willingness to take time out of his busy schedule to point out her failings. In effect she learned to associate conflict and criticism with love. Thus whenever anyone showed interest in her, she felt compelled to test his affection by trying to provoke the familiar parental reaction that she had come to interpret as caring. "If you really care about me," she was unconsciously saying to her lovers, "you'll yell at me like my father."

Her compulsive need to be yelled at satisfied a real and constant longing; it enabled her to re-create a familiar and comfortable past situation in the present even though to an outside observer it seemed very unpleasant. Like the girls who had stayed in Douglaston, she gained something psychologically important to her from a bad situation. She assured herself that no matter how bad things got she would still be welcome at home; she would not have to leap, as Susan did, into the unknown.

The crucial thing to remember is that Barbara did not act freely. She set herself up to repeat self-destructive patterns blindly, as if internally compelled. In psychological terms, we call this a *repetition compulsion*.

It might seem as if Barbara were playing a loser's game. But that's not really true. A repetition compulsion provides some internal satisfaction even though it has negative consequences. Remaining with the familiar causes fewer problems than testing out new ways of relating. For this reason the people involved in most relationships do not try to develop together as a couple so much as they strive to repeat past patterns developed long before they met each other. The familiarity of those patterns produces some comfort despite its long-range inhibiting effect on growth.

Aside from this comfort, there is another reason why people cling to old patterns: they are not always aware they are doing so. Most people have difficulty in recognizing repetition compulsions. Moreover, they generally fail to see how the reactions of others reflect their own actions and reactions; they do not recognize how their own behavior patterns, programmed in the past, create unwanted reactions in others.

Patterns of relating to others remain relatively fixed from early childhood on and constitute an integral part of a person's sense of self. Challenges to these patterns therefore can lead to intense friction and defensiveness. This applies to religious principles, to your sense of obligation to your parents and relatives, to attitudes toward work, and to viewpoints about relationships and marriage itself. People react defensively to any criticism of these built-in attitudes. Yet as relationships evolve, they suffer increasingly from the conflicts caused by contradictory basic attitudes until they develop their own set of repetitive patterns within the relationships themselves.

Dependency patterns, rooted in unresolved ties to parents, generally account for a large portion of these repetitive patterns. A marriage of one or two dependent partners may look very "loving" until these compulsive dependency patterns surface. If, for example, one or both partners have failed to achieve complete independence, they may experience difficulty in communication of intimacy as well as in efforts to be autonomous. Because of compulsive, exaggerated dependency needs, they may take turns infringing on each other's psychological freedom.

This is easily observed in relationships in which the compulsive need to maintain stability leads to the suppression of true feelings. People who grow up in homes that value calmness and the masking of feelings are often reluctant to express feelings openly for fear of rejection. Such was the case with Betty and Bob, who came to me seeking to understand their inability to share their positive as well as negative feelings.

In a session of "couples therapy," I invited them to discuss some of their concerns.

Betty: When I get mad at you and I yell at you, you become withdrawn. Then I feel hurt and guilty. I feel responsible for your sadness. But you never get mad at me.

Bob: I'm angry but I don't know how to express it verbally. I don't know how to deal with it.

Betty: When you withdraw, I don't really know how you're feeling. That makes me crazy. I sulk, and you act as if everything's OK, as if nothing happened. Why does everything have to be OK?

Bob: I enjoy things being OK.

Clearly they both preferred not to face their discomfort so as to understand the reasons for it. The failure to acknowledge their feelings created a continual sense of insecurity in both of them and set the stage for the next bout of conflict.

I asked them to talk about a specific time when conflict evolved from their characteristic styles of suppressing the expression of feelings.

Betty: You were putting up a towel bar and I was rushing you. You were really angry that I was rushing you. I was angry that you wouldn't tell me that you were angry.

Bob: I was mad, but I didn't feel like stopping and leaving until I finished it. So I tried to put you off.

Betty: I could have dealt with it better if you said "get

off my back." It's difficult to deal with your explanations. It would be better if you would say how you were feeling.

Bob: But that's hard to do. It's a pattern I've gotten into. I stay away from uncomfortable feelings. I hold it in.

Betty: That drives me wild. I think you know how I'm feeling and that gets me mad too.

Bob: If you were so mad, why didn't you just say so?

Betty: I was afraid to have a fight about that towel rack. I anticipated so much discomfort that I couldn't fight to change the towel rack. It wasn't worth it to me to deal with what I anticipated your reaction would be. You could have gotten really mad and torn the rack out of the holes.

Bob: You have a tendency to goad me on.

Betty: Because I want to get a rise out of you. I'll keep going. Until you lose your cool.

The mutual dependency fostered by marriage may actually exacerbate unresolved problems people bring to a relationship. This emerges with particular clarity when one partner's compulsion does not form a good fit with the other's.

Conflicting Compulsions

Repetitive patterns can be the source of interpersonal conflict even when they seem to "fit" within the context of the relationship. Consider, for example, the case of a man imitating his dominant father by browbeating his wife who has copied her mother's submissive patterns. However comfortable both may be with these familiar roles, they lack the flexibility to allow each other, or the relationship itself, to grow. As a result, depending on the extent of these compulsive "fits" within the relationship, people experience varying degrees of conflict, tension, and incompatibility because *repetition in itself cannot help you develop mutually satisfying ways to cope with the changes that unions inevitably undergo.*

Severe problems may develop if lovers' compulsions do not fit well together. The different "languages" people learn as children lead to numerous communication problems and those can be quite complex in the case of people with radically different past experiences and expectations.

Henry, for example, visited my office expressing great anxiety about his ability to measure up to his fiancée's increasing demands for attention since they had taken an apartment together. Gloria had been the only child born to a mother who had silently suffered while caring for an alcoholic husband. Henry had been the youngest of three children born to a relatively happy couple whose mutually respectful relationship balanced their individual interests.

Initially everything went well. Gloria satisfied Henry's need to be cared for, and Henry satisfied Gloria's need to baby someone. While they meshed at first, though, the patterns of the past gradually surfaced as they became more involved with each other in day-to-day interaction. As Henry's need for independence grew, he began to interpret her caring behavior as controlling behavior motivated by her need to protect her own dependency.

Soon their divergent expectations began to clash. As the baby of his original family, Henry expected to be pampered and given his own way. Willing to meet some of these needs, Gloria could not meet them precisely as he had experienced them during his childhood. She could not give him the total, unconditional love, or the free hand, that he expected. And when she began to assert her own need to be coddled, he felt her to be pressuring him, and he rebelled.

This relationship illustrates what Eric Berne, in *Games People Play*, called the "Child-Child" interaction. Unable to become involved on a rational, adult basis, each partner insists on repeating familiar, though uncomfortable, patterns from childhood. Each expects to be treated as they were when children, and as a result they both end up dissatisfied. When two people relate to each other in this compulsive manner, they limit their chances of dealing effectively with the present.

Despite the strength of their habitual patterns, Henry and Gloria had to learn that they could draw on a capacity for change and individual action in order to continue to live together. Gloria could not continue to act as if worrying about him were an unfamiliar burden, and Henry could not continue to demand both the attention and the freedom that had been his right as the youngest of his original family. Both of them, in short, had to learn more mature ways of relating to each other.

Birth-Order Problems

The above story illustrates the general truth that "the child is father of the man" and the more specific fact that early family experiences hold the key to understanding current relationships. On one level conflict between Henry and Gloria can be viewed as the result of an only child being unable to cope with the excessive demands of a dependent spouse; but it must be remembered that this is only one way of analyzing the origin of their conflicts.

Understanding how children of different birth orders learn to behave helps explain the difficulties experienced in particular birth-order matches.

The following generalizations are based on clinical observations I have made over the past fifteen years in my efforts to understand the relationship between birth order and subsequent attitudes and styles of relating to others.

1. The Only Child

The only child grows up in an atmosphere defined largely by the needs and wishes of adults. In the home, these children learn to behave in a fashion that will please or impress their elders and have contact with people of their own age only outside of the family home. Thus they learn very early to act like little adults, a pattern with obvious implications for their future lives and relationships. The subsequent relational problems of only children stem from their perfectionistic striving to be like the model adults around them. As adults, the only children tend to be intolerant of less mature mates, insensitive to both their own and other people's failings, and insistent on particularly high standards in both behavior and achievement.

A disproportionately large number of only children become successful writers, statesmen, and performers. But this high achievement rate often costs dearly, for the need to excel, a hallmark of the only child personality, often puts such pressure on these people that it sometimes becomes very difficult for them to get along with other people, and especially with those close to them. Quick to spot less-than-perfect behavior, they often turn their criticism on loved ones who do not share their exacting standards—with predictably unhappy results. And because of their exacting natures, they sometimes cannot ask for help when they need it.

Not only were only children the oldest children in their original families; they were also the youngest—and as such often had things done for them. As a result, many only children fail to develop skills at expressing their need for help, or else they learn to ask for help in an authoritative, "little adult" manner that belies the helplessness or dependency they may be feeling.

Frequently, only children, who repress their dependency needs, blow up or break apart when the strain of that repression gets too severe. If you marry an only child, you must learn to be sensitive to unstated needs: often your partner has not learned how to ask for help or ask to be held. You must recognize that certain demands mask dependent needs; you have to translate their demands to respond to their needs, and learn to quell your inclination to become defensive in response to what may be expressed in authoritative tones.

One young couple, Paul and Norma, were locked into very fixed roles in their relationship as a result of their earliest sibling experiences. Paul, an only child, insisted that Norma do all the things his mother did—including taking care of his clothing, making the food, and paying the bills. Having been "dumped on" by her older brother since childhood, Norma characteristically rebelled by doing a bad job of meeting Paul's demands. Because of his narcissistic preoccupation with himself, Paul could meet few of her needs, and this led her to turn to drugs and alcohol—which invited his attention, although in a critical way.

Lacking the courage to become autonomous, neither of them could move toward independent action. If she were the kind of person who had had experience taking care of the needs of others rather than simply expecting others to take care of her, she could probably have met some of his needs and in turn discovered his capacity to care for her needs, but unfortunately she lacked this capacity. She couldn't get close to him sexually, and he stubbornly remained aloof and critical of her. Only when they functioned as parents did they find some common ground for relating, but this generally occurred only at times of crisis.

Their relationship could not evolve toward mutual interdependence and showed little of the kinds of fluctuations of coming together and separating and growth characteristics of other relationships. They increasingly involved other people in their lives and continued to function in a helpless, dependent fashion toward the outside world.

Treatment focused on helping them see how they contributed to the crises they experienced. They were encouraged to plan mutually agreed upon activities that reduced the need to manipulate each other and diminished the frequency of explosive episodes. In time they established a working relationship in which they were able to head off impending crises by recognizing and controlling the particular types of behavior that had previously led to conflict.

2. The First Born

Like the only child, first-born children frequently become high achievers who often fail to be satisfied with their achievements. Every first born begins life as an only child, which accounts for such personality characteristics as perfectionism and muted dependency.

But the first born has a special problem that the only child does not have. He or she, usually at the age of two or three, has to contend with the arrival of a younger sibling who steals center stage away. This causes varying degrees of resentment in first borns, and is the beginning of what later blossoms into sibling rivalry.

Issues of power and decision making cause conflict for first borns. Despite grandiose fantasies of control and achievement, they disguise their aggressiveness by frequently hiding behind a mask of shyness or selflessness. In addition, many first borns have considerable conflict about their dependency needs, a pattern described in the last chapter.

The first son or daughter grows up with the responsibility of being the "older and wiser" sibling, which often creates difficulties in future relationships. First children want to prove themselves responsible for their mates, yet have an aversion to looking bossy or forward. This usually results from crossed parental signals in which Monday's dictum might be "Take care of your little brother" and Tuesday's is "Stop trying to boss him around."

Many of my first-born patients exhibit a distinctive confusion about their role as the "older and wiser" member of their relationships. Typically they feel themselves to be very sensitive to their partners' needs—while their partners often feel slighted and neglected by them! The first born's difficulty in demonstrating his or her concern clearly stems from the ambivalent stand he or she has had to adopt in the early home environment. First borns need partners who can read nonverbal cues well enough to know when silence really means insensitivity and when it means reluctance to take responsibility. Unfortunately many first borns build relationships with people who want to be taken care of but who at the same time resent the firm hand they seek.

Many first borns learn to maintain a certain distance between themselves and others even though intellectually and emotionally they might want to relate more intimately. The need to maintain this distance conflicts with the need to have closer relationships and can be resolved only by understanding the necessity for both autonomy and intimacy, which are mutually reinforcing. To be intimate you need to be autonomous. To be autonomous, you need intimacy. You have to be able to move in and out of both of those conditions and you can do it only in a relationship in which there is a high tolerance of individuality. This requires a working through of all the problems that occur when people get too close and hang on to each other without letting go. The stress associated with this situation may be one of the reasons for keeping the distance, since the distance enables you to avoid the problems of jealousy, possessiveness, or dependency.

As Susan, a first born, told me: "I tend to be stronger than the men I know. I love being by myself. On the other hand, I feel very lonely sometimes."

Susan fears the loss of her autonomy to a man who will try to control her. For this reason she approaches all relationships casually and is regularly disappointed that they don't develop into more satisfying experiences. But she is reluctant to acknowledge her own dependency needs for fear that she will be controlled. These dependency needs end up being expressed in terms of feelings of loneliness and rage at being treated so casually.

The therapeutic task has been to help her to understand her own needs for dependency and the ability to be confident about her independence so that she can share in a relationship rather than be manipulated or to manipulate in turn.

3. The Second Born

Generally speaking, parents make fewer demands on second-born and middle children than they do on first arrivals. This means that second borns usually feel less pressure to excel, and can develop more reasonable life objectives for themselves than their more exacting older siblings. Their older siblings provide standards of excellence against which they can measure their own potential. Older siblings also demonstrate the possibilities that exist, which enhances the second borns' reality-testing ability. Sometimes this leads to invidious comparison, but generally they can learn from Big Brother's or Big Sister's mistakes, and be more discerning and careful in their own lives. Ultimately this may make them easier to get along with in romantic relationships.

The second born has some vulnerable points as well. Second borns often repress hostility and second sons often either adopt defensive, macho patterns in order to demonstrate that they are just as good as the first child, or display a need to prove themselves in areas untraveled by the first born. But by and large their need to excel is balanced by a cautious or pragmatic approach to realistic goals.

The arrival of a third child—which makes the second born a middle child—increases his or her problems because he or she must learn to be not only appropriately respectful of the elder but also appropriately caring for the younger child. This balance can be difficult to maintain. In very supportive families, the middle child may develop great competence in dealing with a variety of personal interactions. In less supportive settings, however, he or she can become confused about the correctness of certain behaviors, and this confusion often carries over into adult relationships, coloring patterns of interpersonal communication. The person involved with a second-born child therefore needs to be aware of the second born's ambivalence about both deference and caring in order to be successful in daily interaction with them.

4. The Last Born

The peculiar problems of last-born children derive from their early history as the babies of their original families. Youngest children often have an ambivalent attitude toward interpersonal contacts as a result of having grown up in a situation where everyone else—siblings as well as parents—is larger and more powerful. They may suspect that others get more love or attention than they do and that they have been left out because of their smaller size and weakness. Yet, accustomed to being cared for by older siblings, they learn a whole range of subtly manipulative behaviors and techniques to ensure that this care will continue.

Typically, youngest children demonstrate much charm, conviviality, and ease with people—perhaps as a result of being pampered and protected. They have skills in getting what they want from others, and often achieve success in fields that value public charm—they excel, for example, as salespersons, promoters, and politicians. Benjamin Franklin, the youngest of nineteen children, clearly demonstrated how a youngest child could manipulate cleverness and charm into success.

A negative aspect of a last born's personality may be an intense need for others to provide care much as the family did. The dependency needs of last borns can be intense, and if thwarted may be transformed into hostile demands that may disrupt their relationships.

Understanding the Past

The four representative sketches of birth-order positions that I have outlined do not exhaust the subtleties of the subject. But they do underscore the principle that early life experiences such as birth order can affect the way you manage your life and your relationships today. Therefore, the more aware you become of how birth position influences the way you and your partner behave, the better able you will be to deal with each other in the present.

Harriet and Gregory, for example, illustrate how two individual styles both complement and disrupt each other. Growing up with a dominating but supportive older brother, Harriet found Gregory's domineering ways both familiar and reassuring, though her marrying him entailed a certain loss of freedom. Gregory tended to control Harriet so as to ensure that she would provide the support and pampering that he had become accustomed to in his childhood, when two older sisters cared for him. The two personalities worked together to create an interaction that benefited both of them.

Yet Gregory complained bitterly about Harriet's lack of self-direction and autonomy—apparently unaware of his contribution to that lack. Comfortable and yet resentful about being pampered, he would poke fun at her in social situations as he had done to his sisters, but without being aware of her embarrassment. For her part, Harriet begrudgingly tolerated Gregory's demands, since they reminded her of her brother's.

This "worked" all right for many years, but when their children reached adolescence, their relationship began to fall apart. Feeling less needed by her children, Harriet began to rebel against Gregory's control. Panicked by her newly developed strength, Gregory became increasingly argumentative and demanding. With considerable time and effort, I helped them to restructure their lives so that they could both enjoy independence while still caring for each other.

This case underscores the compulsive repetition of the behavioral patterns of the past in the present. No matter how unique and special a relationship seems to be, many of its dimensions actually result from these circular repetitive patterns.

Does it follow that you can never break out of the repetitive circle? Does your past patterning make it impossible for you to ever do anything new? Is it true, as J. M. Barrie once observed, that "Nothing we do after we are twelve matters very much?" Most definitely not. However tenaciously they hold on, the roles learned in childhood can be understood and overcome. You can learn to put them aside and learn new ways of interacting with others that go beyond the scripts learned in childhood.

Chapter 8

Scripts and Systems

In chapter 4 I described John and Lucille, a couple whose interaction constantly seesawed between closeness and aloneness. They handled the push-pull of mutuality and autonomy, the central problem of relationships, in a confused way. Instead of maintaining a healthy balance between togetherness and separateness, they remained in a state of continual disequilibrium and tension.

This is not an uncommon pattern. All relationships develop a balance of their own, but in many relationships the inability of the partners to find an emotional space between them disrupts this balance. In fact, the more they try to keep things on an even keel, the more often they seem to create tension: the effort to "firm things up" actually causes even more trouble.

The behavior of one person in a relationship, moreover, almost always elicits a typical, and predictable, response —a reactive behavior—from his or her partner, which keeps the relationship in basically the same interaction pattern. As we saw in the last chapter, most couples who try to change their relationships without analyzing the patterns of their interaction end up repeating those patterns.

Stanford psychiatrist Richard Fisch has illustrated this redundant, closed aspect of relationships with an illuminating image. Imagine, he says, two people joined at the waist by a ten-foot rigid pole that keeps them both together and apart at an unchanging distance. The pole, which serves as both a link and a barrier, dooms them to move with each other through a limited number of predictable patterns.

A self-enclosed system has made them captive:

> In this system it does not matter if either tries to establish more contact, for every advance by one partner is predictably and observably followed by a withdrawal of the other . . . so that every attempt by one partner to come closer pushes the other away, and vice versa, giving rise to endless mutual accusations, but resulting in a wondrous dance in which nothing ever changes.*

Furthermore, within such a system you cannot distinguish cause from effect. Everything functions as both cause *and* effect, since everything done by one partner causes, as well as results from, a set behavior of the other.

Various metaphors characterize the repetitive, self-limiting aspects of relationships. Relationships, for example, can be viewed as designs that exhibit familiar, recurrent *patterns*. Borrowing from information theory, they may be considered closed, or redundant *systems*. Or they can be viewed, in terms of role playing, as an elaborate interpersonal *psychodrama*. This last metaphor, which likens relational conflict to an aspect of an unwritten play, is the one I want to explore in this chapter.

Most people like to think of themselves as independent,

*Paul Watzlawick, John Weakland, and Richard Fisch, *Change* (New York: Norton, 1974), p. 16.

resourceful individuals who write their own "scripts." Such assessments are rarely accurate, though. In fact most people live their lives and experience their relationships in terms of *other* people's scripts. Let's look a little more closely at this unfortunate fact.

Role Confusions

Loving couples most often restrict their own freedom by behaving in terms of *expectations* rather than in terms of their own objectives. As I pointed out in the last chapter, lovers frequently re-enact the scripts from their own childhood experiences rather than create new scripts in terms of present needs. The roles of childhood thus frequently become the roles of adult life. But these personal, family-oriented roles are only one aspect of role playing. Society's roles also impinge on lovers' freedom. Cultural and social role expectations, in fact, at times can be just as stultifying and limiting as the roles learned in family patterns.

Western culture, for example, still promulgates certain rigid notions of correct behavior for men and women, husbands and wives. Focused on cultural role models of "husband" or "wife," loving couples may find it difficult to relate on a satisfactory interpersonal basis. Preoccupied with adhering to their marital roles, they forget how to enjoy being with each other. As the leading lady in the now defunct TV series "United States" told her spouse, "I wish you'd act less like a husband and more like a friend."

Most people find it easier to fill the role of husband or wife than that of friend to their spouse. Friendship means adopting a curious and difficult mixture of straightforwardness and vulnerability, while the role of spouse offers

a much more clearly defined set of behavioral expectations. For many people, being both friend and lover is just
a too ambiguous, spontaneous, taxing, and terrifying role
to play well. The social role, for them, is far more comfortable than the personal role.

Jean Genet's wonderful play about social roles, *The Bal-
cony*, demonstrates with poignant clarity how the use of
a social mask can make social interactions easier than personal interaction. In that play each character wears a cos-
tume that sets the tone for his or her appropriate role
behavior: the Bishop behaves like a bishop, the Politician
behaves like a politician, the Prostitute behaves like a
prostitute, and so on. Genet doesn't give his characters
individual names of personalities, but characterizes them
in terms of *function*, permitting them to act only in socially defined ways. Without their socially defined roles,
the characters have no substance. Genet underscores the
power of social roles in interpersonal relations, and points
out that these roles usually keep people from discovering
the inner qualities both of themselves and of others.

But living out social roles rather than striving for real
communication almost always proves to be an unsatisfying experience. Expecting yourself and your spouse to
behave solely in an appropriate or traditional manner will
lead you to constrict your self-expression, impose unrealistic demands on each other, and usher in many repetitive
manipulations. Too great an adherence to traditional roles
impedes the growth of harmonious development and
communication patterns based on each partner's actual
qualities.

To carry the theatrical metaphor a little further, most
people not only play defined roles most of the time, but
also play the *same* roles over and over again. They not

only try to fit certain roles but are *typecast* in terms of how they will play these roles.

Typecasting has value in the theater and the cinema. It makes for easy recognition and predictable performances. The person typecast as a strong silent hero (like John Wayne, for example) or as a fluttery scatterbrain (like Judy Holliday) need not stretch himself or herself in a role; the audience relates to specific familiar types and expects to experience specific and familiar emotional responses to them.

The emphasis on typecasting and predictable responses may make good commercial sense in the limited world of film making, but it can be disastrous in personal relationships, where role playing and predictable responses can become circular and unproductive.

Throughout twenty years of marriage, Wanda and Sam, for example, had adhered to fixed concepts of marital roles. Raised by a disagreeable stepfather, Sam sought an idealized state of friendship and "being together" in marriage, which he felt he had missed as a child. The ideal wife for him was a good companion, not someone who cared for his needs. He wanted Wanda to do things with him and resented the fact that she was always trying to "boss me around."

Yet like a good stoic he never let her know how he felt, and so resentment generally built up in him and led him to withdraw. Wanda interpreted his withdrawal as rejection, and to make amends, she made active efforts to do more of what she believed would be in keeping with being the "good wife." She had grown up helping her mother care for a sickly but doting father. She believed that a wife's role was to take over and manage things, to envelop her husband with love. Of course, Sam couldn't handle this. Because of confusion over their "proper" marital roles, the two sought my help.

I advised them that they had been playing improper roles, and that they had to learn to talk to each other about their individual hopes and aspirations for the relationship; this would help them to adapt their daily performances to become more mutually supportive.

Unfortunately, few couples talk this way before marriage; instead, they plunge into their mutual play without even giving the script a glance. As a result many of them end up totally confused about their marriage roles, yet unable to get out of the play. This usually proves disastrous. Unless you clarify your concept of your role and your partner's role in the relationship, you may unwittingly impinge on each other and not be able to learn from your mutual experiences. If you are caught in a fixed pattern of role interactions, you won't be able to identify or flow with the feelings you generate in each other. You also may have difficulty viewing your relationship objectively, and will tend to attribute your conflicts to your partner's failure to follow his or her "cues" properly.

This is almost always a serious error—a bad "reading" of the situation, if you like. As I noted in chapter 4, blaming another person for disappointing your expectations can be easier to do than discussing your likes and dislikes, your desires and worries and feelings. You will find it easier to do what comes naturally, what's most automatic and habitual, than to try to understand each situation and respond with more thoughtfulness and reasoning. If your spouse yells at you every time you fail to take out the garbage on time, it's easier to feel offended and blame him for "overreacting" than it is to ask yourself, "How have I provoked this unpleasant response?" It's easier, when your partner pushes you away, to say, "She's just a bitch," than to ask yourself what you've been doing to trigger her response.

Of course it's not possible to analyze everything, and it's quite possible, as I've mentioned before, to overanalyze, but *your behavior is linked* to your spouse's. Certain cues set up certain responses. Your individual responses do not exist in a vacuum but are part of an entire fabric of dialogue; the more you can understand about the internal structure and coherence of that dialogue, the better you will be able to *modify* your own part to elicit responses you want rather than those you don't.

Unlike the script that actors and actresses learn to perform in a play, *your script is not in final form*. It can be changed by you as you desire.

Most people, unfortunately, don't realize this—or if they do realize it, the recognition of possible freedom it gives them is just too much to comprehend, so that rather than experimenting with new lines, they retreat into old familiar roles again—and end up miserable.

If this goes on long enough, the mask may actually take you over. When this occurs, your relationship may "firm up" for good. Without communication about your respective roles and experimentation with different ways of doing things, your *roles* can easily turn into *rules*, locking you into the same repetitions forever.

From Roles to Rules

When Madeline Johnson came to me for help, she had been at war with her husband, Jim, for thirty-five years. Depressed and frustrated by so many years of tension, she described a pattern of marriage based on a repetitive script in which she and her husband always ended up losing.

Basically, neither of the Johnsons felt lovable—yet they avoided any discussion about this central fact, choosing instead to engage in virtually the same dialogue with each other for over three decades. When Madeline expressed warmth for her husband, he would invariably put her down with a humorous dismissal, then draw closer to her with an apology. She in turn would reject him for the dismissal, and the overall pattern of distancing-approach-distancing would continue.

On many occasions, Jim would approach Madeline amorously while she was washing the dishes. "Not now," she would respond. "Wait until I'm finished." Misreading this request as rejection, Jim would withdraw to another room and sulk. Later, when Madeline was ready, she would approach Jim—and he would then invariably reject her. By approaching each other at inconvenient times, they managed to maintain their distance even while they were reaching out.

Their behavior frustrated them even though it was predictable and coherent. Their interchanges occurred in certain *implicit fixed sequences* rather than in haphazard fashion. The rigidity and invariability of these sequences gave them the quality of a set of behavioral rules that they had evolved over the years to organize their relationship.

All relationships develop such sets of repetitive interactional patterns. These patterns become the rules of the relationship, determining what kinds of behavior will be viewed as "fair" and "unfair." While this stabilizes relationships, it becomes a problem when the rules obstruct rather than enhance communication. In Jim and Madeline's case, the unwritten rules codified misunderstanding, and allowed interacting dependencies to feed off each other parasitically rather than nourish each other.

In good relationships, behavioral rules act as *guidelines* to help the couple enjoy each other more fully. In relationships characterized by poor mutuality, or pseudomutality, rules strengthen repetitive neurotic patterns, prohibit free action, and reinforce rote behavior. People respond dutifully to their cues without ever understanding the meaning of the game.

Much psychological literature since Freud has focused on marital unions characterized by predictable patterns of complementary interaction. Psychologists at Stanford's Mental Research Institute have described such relationships in terms of a concept of *rigid complementarity*, in which the interactions create a pathological pattern that transcends the problems of either of the people involved. The unions are composed of individuals "who outside their homes (or otherwise in the absence of their partners) are perfectly capable of functioning satisfactorily, and who, when interviewed individually, may appear very well adjusted. This picture often changes dramatically when they are seen together with their 'complements.' The pathology of their *relationship* then becomes patent."*

With this kind of structure, the "game" can readily take over the players, who become locked into pathological, but familiar, patterns of behavior without being able to see any prospects for change or invention. When the play becomes more important than the players, repetition is inevitable. As Paul Watzlawick put it in another context: "Each marital structure has its own systemic order, its

*Paul Watzlawick, Janet Beavin, and Don Jackson, *Pragmatics of Human Communication* (New York: Norton, 1967), p. 109.

own rules, its own quid pro quo, or 'tacit contract.' Trying to solve conflict within the frame of this contract will inevitably fail."*

Attempts at change invariably fail because they attack only the immediately visible conflicts between the two players, and not the unspoken *contract* at the base of those conflicts. The poor mutuality of Madeline and Jack lasted as long as it did only because neither one of them could step back from the situation and observe the self-defeating nature of their behavior. They could only see a series of alternating rejections. They couldn't see the linkage between one rejection and the next or the fixed sequencing of these rejections. They needed someone outside the relationship to point out the unwritten rules.

Games Without End?

The use of the metaphor of "games" has become quite familiar in the fifteen years since Eric Berne first popularized it in his book *Games People Play*. People talk frequently today about "avoiding games" or "getting beyond games," implying that no self-respecting adult would want to get involved in the vicious childish pastime of playing games. The rejection of social "masks" and the breaking of rigid interactional "rules" have become touchstones of the current self-help literature. The assumption seems to be that if you can drop the polite formulae that grease the social machinery, you'll become a "real" person and get in touch with what you really want to be doing.

Doing this, though, can be difficult, and it's not always

*Watzlawick, Weakland, and Fisch, *Change*, p. 73.

entirely healthy. Indeed, playing some games may be an actual social necessity. Playing them *without realizing what you are doing,* however, may only increase your interpersonal distress. Therefore, you have to *learn the rules* before you agree to go on playing. If you do that, you will be in a better position to play effectively (and honestly) than if you simply behave as Rule No. 3 or Script No. 4 tells you you're supposed to.

Games are the principle modality of social interaction, through which many of us define our psychological needs, nourish our interdependencies, and reassure ourselves that we are fundamentally OK. If not properly learned, games can become incredibly rigid, it is true, but when psychologists speak of social interaction as a series of games, they don't mean that the interaction is therefore trivial, playful, or harmful; they mean simply that most human interaction seems to follow predictable, and recurrent, designs. The clinical concept of games refers simply to "sequences of behavior which are governed by rules."*

It's the *fixed nature* of these sequences that often makes them debilitating. As long as they remain within their particular interactional system, the players can devise no alternatives to it, and therefore come to consider themselves doomed. They cannot win, and they cannot leave the situation. They may have entered their relationships expecting them to turn into blissful dreams: instead they find themselves trapped in nightmares from which they can perceive no escape.

When two people establish the kind of repetitive, non-progressive interaction I've been describing, they may be said to have evolved what the Stanford group has called

Pragmatics, p. 45.

a communal Game Without End. They cannot break its rigid rules because they compulsively apply *first-order* solutions to problems requiring *second-order* change.*

A first-order solution follows the rules, and "occurs within a given system which itself remains unchanged"; a second-order solution transmutes the rules, and "changes the system itself."† Second-order change, then, enables you to distance yourself from the pathological or self-destructive system of rules that you and your partner have agreed unconsciously to follow. The second-order change enables you to step outside the game and *communicate* about it. Only by doing this can you ultimately stop the game, turn your Games Without End into opportunities for change and self-reflection—and, finally, invent your own games, and your own system.

Your Own System

Thoreau observed that most people "lead lives of quiet desperation," and if you look around you, you will see even the happiest people are never quite content, never quite doing what they want to be doing, but instead are dutifully following other people's prescriptions for leading their lives. This is especially true of close relationships, which often capture the minds of the involved people, transforming them into mere pawns of their own interactions. For most people, patterns, roles, and rules are more significant than real interpersonal expression. First-order change, which reinforces the existing systems, is the norm: second-order change, for most couples, seems almost out of reach.

*Change, p. 10; *Pragmatics*, pp. 232–36.
†Change, p. 10.

But it need not be out of reach. I believe couples can escape the rigid patterning that develops from their interactions, and in the following chapters I'll outline specific techniques for learning how to do this. Here I want to outline only a few general principles on which fruitful interactional change must be based.

First of all, to change the way you interact with your partner, you must first understand the rules of your current relationship. By examining in detail how you typically behave with each other, you can discern, within your mutual behavior, those recurrent patterns that might be limiting your potential for growth.

In other words, the first step toward any change is to *determine the implicit rules* in your relationship, i.e., the fixed sequences of behavior that limit the range, diversity, and flexibility of your responses. Consider, for example, typical sequences of communication (who says what to whom), how decisions are made, and whose priorities usually take precedence. A recognition of the *regularities* in your relationship is essential before you can begin to overcome difficulties.

The best way to begin this is by talking. In this connection, pay attention not only to what you discuss with your partner but also to the *manner* in which you relate to each other. The more familiar you become with the rules of the relationship, the better you'll be able to manage conflict. You can learn to be in tune with your spouse, learn when to shift gears, and when to be more sympathetic.

By becoming aware of the nonverbal dimensions of communication, you can learn how your predetermined attitudes and expectations create certain scenarios or scripts that organize events into characteristic trigger situations, and arrange typical sequencings of incidents into full-blown conflicts. By becoming more conscious of these things, you'll develop a greater control over the relationship as a whole.

The mutual expression and acceptance of frailty and unpleasantness as well as the mutual appreciation of strength and joy build successful unions. To help people learn to exchange honest emotions, I generally ask couples who visit my office to discuss their problems with each other in the same way as they typically do at home. Drawing their attention to the interaction patterns becomes the goal of therapy. To the extent that they can gain some perspective on these patterns, they can develop greater awareness and control over conflict.

I do not advocate "shouting matches" every time your partner gets on your nerves. The survival of any friendship depends on a certain amount of restraint and an awareness that *how* you say something can be more important than *what* you say. Indeed, a couple may argue about a dozen different topics and yet sustain the same basic interactional pattern throughout: the rules of the relationship govern the *manner* as well as the *matter* of your exchanges, and as such you should identify consistent patterns of tone and nuance as well as repetitive exchanges of meaning. If you fail to do that, you may end up simply substituting one touchy subject for another, and go on yelling at each other all the same. This would be an example of bringing a first-order change to a second-order dilemma.

Finally, improvisation will help keep a loving union alive.

At one of my Life Strategy Workshops, we sometimes ask participants to behave as if they were a palm tree, an exercise that makes the individual aware of a range of behavior available to him or her that does not fit into the prescribed patterns. We employ this kind of exercise frequently, as a way of helping people to learn to be at ease before groups and also as a way of shaking up preconceptions about the nature of a "role," or a "script."

I'm not suggesting that you imagine yourself to be a palm tree the next time you and your partner have a fight, unless of course that jogs your imagination to react in a newly improvised fashion. I am suggesting that you can use improvisational techniques in your interactions every day, as a way of relating to your lover that had not been designed for you beforehand. Instead of playing your usual role of "husband" or "loving father" or "career woman," I suggest you try to deal with your mate directly, as one person to another.

Now, to do this may generate a great deal of anxiety. Unfamiliarity is frightening and is the reason that most people prefer not to improvise in their relationships but to run through the same scripts over and over. If you are forced to improvise without your customary rules and roles, though, your capacity to communicate might become inventive and rich. Experiences might occur in the context of this workshop relationship that could not have occurred before. You might find things out about yourself that you had never imagined before. You might feel awkward, shy, or foolish, but you would have a chance to learn about the communication of feelings, and this might prove a healthy opportunity for growth. If you kept at it, if you and your spouse continued to work at the communication of feelings rather than acting in terms of fixed roles, you would gradually develop your own system in which, because you were conscious of what you were doing, you both ceased to be pawns and instead become masters of your shared destiny.

The English poet William Blake (who stayed happily married to the same woman for forty-five years), once noted, "I must create my own system or be enslaved by an other man's." That's an idea with great relevance for the management of interpersonal tension. The couples who cope best with the ups and downs of close unions have come to understand the fixed sequences of their interchanges, and have tried to change those sequences— to write their own rules—so that they nourish each others' strengths rather than weaknesses, and become truly cooperative rather than merely complementary. Such couples refuse to be enchained by the fixed systems of the past. Like Blake, they design and live their own lives.

How can you join that happy company? The principles I've outlined here will, I hope, be of help. In the last chapters of the book I want to focus more specifically on how you can master your relationships rather than be victimized by them. The techniques presented in the following chapters will help you develop your capacity for second-order change, which in turn will help you devise your own interpersonal system—one that can absorb and transmute conflict—because it is truly your own.

Chapter 9

Metacommunication

The fable about the blind men and the elephant stands out as a superb illustration of the basic dilemma inherent in human communication. Three blind men in search of shelter bumped into an elephant. In an effort to identify the obstacle, they reached out and began to touch it in various places.

The first man touched one of the elephant's legs and concluded that it felt like a tree.

The second man reached out and touched the elephant's trunk. "No," he replied. "It feels more like a snake."

The third man reached out and ran his hand up and down the elephant's side. "You are both wrong," he announced. "This is a house."

In reality, an elephant does not resemble a tree, a snake, or a house, but the blind men could not be convinced of that. Nor could they convince one another of the validity of their individual impressions. Holding to their views, none of them learned anything about the elephant, or even corrected their own small, limited view of the larger reality.

If they had agreed to cooperate—if each man had been receptive to the other men's impressions as well as his own—they might have formed a more accurate picture. But they refused to consider anything but their own data and thus remained ignorant.

Most people in relationships behave like the blind men in the story. Faced with conflict or the necessity of change, they refuse to consider other perspectives. They hold fast to their own myopic views, and end up no better informed about their dilemmas than the blind men were about the elephant.

As noted in the last chapter, couples interact in predictable and recurring ways, staying with the familiar rather than trying out new ways of feeling and behaving. Trouble arises when they become locked into the roles associated with these patterns. Failing to see the fixed quality of their roles and interaction patterns, they believe they have the freedom to act as they wish and tend to withdraw into shells or blame their partners for problems caused by the relationship itself.

Relationships that regress to this point often devolve into noncommunicative systems characterized by shouting matches. Like the blind men, people in such unions don't care about finding a solution for their problems, only about holding on to their private versions of reality. Ironically, this sometimes occurs in an atmosphere of constant conversation. But rather than actually communicating, people who compete with each other in their relationships prefer to match insights continually, even if it means that nothing is understood.

Contest of Wits

Stepping back from a situation, assessing it objectively, and comparing your view with your partner's view can be difficult once conflict exists. More than likely you will find it easier to firm up your own view, rejecting or discounting other viewpoints. However, once you do this, it becomes even more difficult to drop your defenses, give in, and appreciate the other person's viewpoint. As long as you see your partner as a rival rather than a friend, and your discussions as battles rather than interchanges, it will be difficult to reduce conflict through communication because of the inclination to view acceptance of the other person's viewpoint as a surrender of your own position. Too often communication serves the purpose of competition and an effort to score points against each other. This may gratify your ego for a time, but it will inevitably wreak havoc on your union.

I once helped a young couple overcome such a communicational impasse. Peter and Vivian seemed to be more in love with words than with each other. They expressed their feelings in the most eloquent and precise terms imaginable, yet they made little or no effort to consider how they sounded to each other. As a result they got bogged down in verbiage instead of really trading ideas.

Peter regularly quoted poetry, and Vivian had read every psychological monograph ever written, but they used their intellectual achievements in self-protective ways rather than to enrich their lives—throwing *bons mots* at each other and totting up scores instead of trying to understand each other. In one exchange Vivian accused Peter of ignoring her.

"You're in your own little world," she said.

"I can't help that," he replied. "The mind is its own place."

"That's a devil of a way to see things," Vivian responded, and for a moment they both smiled, as if they had just shared an arcane, private joke.

"What are you two talking about?" I asked.

Vivian smirked. "Peter likes to throw out a little Milton now and then," she said, "to see if I remember the lines."

"That was *Paradise Lost,*" added Peter. "The devil that Vivian mentioned speaks that line in the poem."

They both looked pleased, even though their communication problems seemed far from being resolved. Peter had quoted Milton to get "one up" on Vivian, and she had countered by alluding to the poem herself, demonstrating her cleverness at not being stumped. Obviously, they both derived satisfaction from this exchange, but on a deeper level it only served to keep them apart.

"Do you think," I asked, "that this kind of literary contest gets you closer or keeps you farther apart? Do you really want to change?"

They did want to change their relationship in order to interact in a more satisfying way. With some effort they began to see that their intellectual competitions impeded the communication process rather than improving it. Gradually, as they learned to communicate in simple and direct terms rather than in the highly abstract and allusive manner they had learned in academia, their relationship began to improve.

Even though few people can quote Milton at will, most of them spend some energy trying simultaneously to impress and put down their partners. This leads inevitably to conflict-laden discussions that often resemble college debates more than intimate communications.

The participants in a debate do not seek truth, nor must they even believe their argument. They merely try to argue their side's case effectively. It doesn't matter whether you support a particular issue. If you draw the *con* slip, you must try to defend that viewpoint as vigorously as you would have defended the *pro* position if you had drawn it.

Debating contests help in the development of good argumentative strategies, but don't necessarily help the pursuit of wisdom, harmony, or truth. Debating societies, in general, serve as training grounds for future lawyers and politicians, and they therefore view discussion as an opportunity for besting an opponent: the entire advocacy structure of the law, as well as the election structure of our political system, demands that the players in politics and law become adept at witty exchange and logical, coherent defense. However, dedication to the unalloyed facts at hand does not constitute an essential part of their training.

Dedication to the facts, however, does constitute an essential part of an ongoing relationship. A good relationship cannot be merely a lifelong contest, geared toward deflating contrary arguments and one-upping an opponent. Relationships based on such exchanges have very little chance of long-term survival. Real intimacy, like real autonomy, grows from mutual respect and a readiness to resolve the inevitable conflicts of living together to achieve a shared freedom. Verbal cleverness often obscures mutual respect and impedes this complex process.

Attempting to defend your own version of the truth at all costs, therefore, can create confusion. Unlike elephants, relationships are constantly changing, in part because of your reactions to and impact on the relationship. The blind man touching the elephant's trunk does not thereby turn the elephant into a snake; but you may well transform your relationship into something unexpected and unmanageable by how you view it and talk about it.

In other words, a relationship does not have tangible or

fixed qualities that remain set forever. It is created anew all the time. You make reality every day. Moreover, you cannot do this alone or unilaterally, but must do it in concert (amiable or troubled) with your partner. If you can learn to cooperate and exchange real feelings, you'll have a far better chance of keeping your love alive than if you insist on having your view accepted at all times.

Communication in this way can be difficult. Human beings, as we have seen, bring unresolved tensions and past experiences to their relationships, and these often get in the way of real exchange. Sensitivity to the common patterns that obstruct good communication can therefore be helpful.

Bad Communication Patterns

Paranoid tendencies, low frustration tolerance, poor control of anger, and the need for immediate gratification have powerful and negative effects on others, and on the quality of relationships. Once you respond with one of these typical obstructive behaviors, you increase the likelihood that your partner will misinterpret, exaggerate, or distort the nature of his or her response. People tend not to realize that their actions and manner of presenting themselves to others define them; whether they want to or not, they communicate to others the discrepancies between how they feel and how they act. The discordances between your feelings and your behavior may convey a confused and ambiguous message to others, who may respond to different aspects of your behavior than the ones that you think you're transmitting.

For this reason, it's important to determine *exactly what has been said to you* in any interpersonal situation, and not just what seems to be said. A narcissistic individual will be inclined to interpret all behavior in personal terms, and will be inclined to express some parancia at the slightest indication of rejection, negativism, or criticism. He or she may also want his or her needs met constantly, and may display insensitivity to those of others. If you can spot this kind of problem, you will be able to resolve conflicts in your relationship more realistically.

This can be difficult to do. As I noted earlier in the chapter, people generally interpret interactions in their own terms, and only reluctantly see things from other people's viewpoints. In chapter 5, I discussed the fear of intimacy as it related to one couple, Helen and Paul.

Paul's reluctance to be warm to Helen and her demanding need to control the relationship were both examples of self-centered behaviors that created a communicational impasse. Locked into predictable and self-defeating roles, they exchanged loaded messages with each other, which only intensified Paul's passivity and Helen's anger.

On one occasion they reiterated a typical argument about leaving a party.

"I didn't care," said Paul. "I just let her decide. It wasn't a big issue for me."

"But you resented it, all the same. You know you did. You resented me making the decision. I said, 'Let's go,' and so we went, and you got steamed up about it. It would have been the same if we'd stayed."

"I wasn't feeling that hostile," Paul defended himself. "I only got mad at you after you got mad at me."

"You were sulking, and you know it. He sulked all the way home. Naturally I got pissed off. Who can take all that damn silence. So I said, 'What's wrong?' and he blew up at me."

"It was the *way* that you said it. Like an attack, not really caring how I felt."

At this point I directed their attention to the fact that, in their description of the episode, they seemed to be recapitulating the same patterns of communication that had led to the blowup in the first place. They were, in fact, about to blow up again. So, the issue of returning home had less significance than the underlying pattern of derogation, mutual accusation, and the inability to recognize the imact of their *manner* of communication.

Neither Paul nor Helen recognized the strong nonverbal cues and interactions that they communicated to each other. Paul generally slumped in the chair and directed his eyes at the floor when he spoke to Helen. Helen, by contrast, characteristically gestured toward Paul, throwing out her hand as if to reach out to him. Paul interpreted this as an attack.

Their pattern resembled that of most couples who don't listen. They don't listen to verbal or nonverbal communication, they don't listen to the sounds of words, they don't listen to their meanings. They ignore tone of voice and body language signals, and yet these often convey a great deal of information about feelings and attitudes. Becoming aware of these unspoken signals can enhance your relationship.

Tuning In

The best communication patterns fill mutually agreed upon needs and do not merely reflect automatic behavior patterns rooted in the past. But such communication requires considerable effort: it's seldom easy to become aware of your needs, express them without fear of ridicule, and listen to the needs of your partner so as to fine-tune both sets of needs. Most people focus on the *literal* meaning of words rather than their overall meaning. Few people agree about their verbal communications, let alone their nonverbal or attitudinal communications systems. Moreover, few attempt to develop and agree upon a set of rules to effectively change bad communication patterns.

Unfortunately, most communication occurs nonverbally. Although it takes time to tune in to nonverbal patterns, you must do it to avoid repeating unhealthy patterns.

You can learn to tune in to nonverbal cues by focusing on how you react to your partner as well as on your choice of words and tone. You can focus on your body language as well by becoming aware of your body movements, or what Julius Fast has called kinesics.* Finally, you can focus on a wide range of communicational signals, including:

> posture, gesture, facial expression, voice inflection, the sequence, rhythm and cadence of the words themselves, and any other nonverbal manifestation of which the organism is capable, as well as the communicational clues unfailingly present in any *context* in which an interaction takes place.†

Nonverbal communication covers a wide range of behavior. Tuning into it really constitutes learning a whole new language of nonverbal communication—more complicated, less precise, but also inestimably richer in nuance than purely verbal languages.

Naturally, most people are reluctant to learn this new

*See, for example, Julius Fast, *Body Language* (New York: Pocket Books, 1971).

†Watzlawick, Beavin, and Jackson, *Pragmatics of Human Communication* (New York: Norton, 1967), p. 62.

language. Recently I conducted a family counseling session with the parents of Margaret, a young woman who had been telling me for weeks that she and her parents didn't communicate. After entering the office, her father sat down at one end of the room, hunched into the chair, and began to glower. Her mother sat at the other end, shaking her head and sighing. Margaret sat in the middle, looking from side to side. Neither parent seemed to recognize Margaret's discomfort or their role in contributing to it. They had not developed the capacity to read each other's *metalanguage*, and therefore could not apprehend (consciously) the unpleasantness of the situation.

One exchange made this clear. Commenting on his concern for her mental health, Margaret's father reported how difficult it had been for him to get her to shut off the lights in their house. As he spoke, he sounded as if he were describing a barely mentionable crime. His muscles tightened, his brows knit, his face became florid, and his voice sounded biting and constricted.

"You sound pretty angry," I said.

"Angry? No," he responded. "I just don't like to waste money."

He angrily denied that he was angry, focusing instead on the economics and reasonableness of his demands, and demonstrating almost total unawareness of his negative and inhibiting effect on his daughter. When I called his attention to the possibility that he might be communicating rage to his daughter without realizing it, he again denied it by saying: "We love each other. We never get angry in our house."

This sad, and unfortunately all too common, case of a self-imposed communicational block clearly contributed to Margaret's chronic feelings of inadequacy, her confusion, and her inclination to avoid close relationships for fear of rejection. Her tearful withdrawal only served to intensify his anger, and yet he could not comprehend that he had brought about her response. This enabled him to justify his critical attitude toward her, even though it had effectively led to almost a total breakdown of communication between them.

How do you tune into nonverbal levels of communication? How, without the objective input of a therapist or a trained observer, can you recognize the elements of nonverbal interaction that strain your relationship?

Developing a system of metacommunication—that is, of talking about *how* you talk—can be difficult, since it entails awareness of verbal and nonverbal communication as well as some understanding of your characteristic scripts and scenarios.

The rhythms and cadences of interaction patterns, that convey instructions to others as to what they should do with the information being transmitted, can be so elusive that people often need the help of a therapist to become aware of even the simplest sequencing of body language, gesture, and tone.

What if you don't have a therapist? What if your conflict has not proceeded to the point yet that you feel you need professional help? Is there anything you can do personally, on your own initiative, to tune in better to each other and become more sensitive to the invisible structural framework in which your communications are imbedded?

Questions to Ask Yourself

There are two steps to take in improving your relationship on your own. The first step is to examine basic communication patterns in your relationship. The second is to apply certain techniques for analyzing communication in new ways so as to help you to master not just the obvious, verbal messages but also the less obvious undercurrents as well.

Those are general steps. Specifically, you might want to ask yourself a number of questions:

1. Are you critical rather than constructive in your comments to others? Perhaps what you regard as logical and pragmatic may be viewed by others as hostile and controlling. You may size up situations very easily without being aware that your sense of certainty annoys your spouse, or you may come across with a smug, self-confident manner and tone that trigger defensive behavior in people who will not accept your "logic."

2. Do you think of yourself as helpful but find that others experience your helpfulness as controlling behavior? Do you make others feel helpless and inadequate with your helpfulness?

3. Conversely, do you induce guilt by virtue of your helplessness? Do people constantly apologize to you, or go overboard trying to please you? If so, consider whether or not you elicit these responses by expressing helplessness. Or do you invite people to feel responsible for the fact that you feel helpless? Do you make them feel guilty and resentful as well? Understanding how dissatisfaction with yourself can burden others can be a step in overcoming such behavior.

4. Do you communicate a feeling of withdrawal or rejection by *not* asking for help even when you genuinely need it? Are you simply too shy or too embarrassed to request assistance from your friends, thinking that the request will be an imposition on them? A reluctance to reach out for help can intensify feelings of isolation, loneli-

ness, and withdrawal, but others may interpret this as evidence of arrogance, not fear. While it takes considerable effort to reach out to others, the self-sufficient stance ultimately creates more distance than before, and makes it all the more difficult for those who might really care about you to express their concern. Don't push yourself on others, but don't be afraid to ask for help when you need it, either.

5. Are you too accepting of the demands of others and too dismissive of your own needs? Do you say yes when you mean no? Are you afraid to say no for fear of disappointing others or incurring their wrath? If so, you must recognize the negative consequences of acting contrary to the way you are feeling: this can lead to the buildup of resentment and tension. If you become too compliant to the demands and expectations of your loved one, you can easily end up as a permanent victim of his or her whims, and not as an equal with your own moods and expectations. You must try to learn what your own needs are and try to develop the courage to draw certain lines. Being nice to somebody doesn't mean that you should ignore your own needs and desires. If you do that, you'll end up feeling just as frustrated as the person you've been trying so hard to "please."

6. Are you transmitting double messages? Do you contradict your verbal messages with nonverbal messages or body language? Do you present yourself clearly, or are you conveying conflicting messages by verbal and nonverbal means? You can seriously confuse others if you smile when you are angry, or reassure them with pointed or double-edged remarks.

7. Do you act as if your loved one can read your mind? Do you reject people when they don't act the way that

you think they should act, even though you haven't told them so? Do you let them know what you expect of them, or do you assume that they should know your needs without being told? Do you often find yourself in a situation with others in which you end up in the linguistic conundrum of saying, "I know you think I know that you know what I think you're thinking, but . . ."? You have to realize that nobody can read your mind. The only way out of such communication impasses is to *say what you mean.*

8. Do you *listen* to others or simply assume you know what they will say before they say it? Do you defensively attach your own meaning to what they are saying, so you don't really hear the nuances of their communication?

If you consider these questions periodically, you will gain some insight into ways in which you may be complicating your communication. Next you will want to learn a few simple techniques to help you to improve communication.

Mastering the Undercurrent

A number of techniques can be used to enhance interpersonal communication. Several specifically address metacommunicational issues. Remember the metaphor of the canoe tossing about in the white water. Learning to manage your actual, verbal language is equivalent, within the bounds of this metaphor, to learning to ride with the surface waves. Knowing how to deal with metacommunication is equivalent to mastering the tricky undercurrent. It's in that undercurrent that most relationships come to final grief, for navigating the unseen and unstated can be a far more difficult task than merely learning a new way of using the words you already know.

Yet it's not an impossible task, and it's one that can be learned with practice. To give you just a few examples, a few techniques for dealing with the swirling beneath the surface, here are some things to keep in mind whenever you experience conflict with your loved one.

1. *Don't keep score.* I once asked a couple who had been married pretty happily for over forty years how they managed to get along with each other for so long. "It's simple," they said. "We don't keep score."

A good working relationship is based not on rivalry but on cooperation. This means that such a union's dominant mode of communication must be based on a desire not to score points against an opponent, but to work together toward a mutually satisfying interaction. To keep your love alive, you must go beyond the contests and games to a place where there are no winners or losers, no prizes or black marks or scores.

Real communication begins only when you realize that it's a two-way street—and when you begin to talk not only about the specific issues of the day-to-day, but about the *way* you typically interact. Real communication is meta-communication, or communication *about* communication.

2. The primary focus in a good relationship should not be your version or your partner's version of reality, but a shared understanding of how your joint participation itself creates reality for the two of you.

Polarization may occur if you try too hard to convince your spouse of the unreasonableness of his or her viewpoint. But if the two of you, working together with an awareness of your unique separateness, can create a *shared* version of reality that acknowledges your failings as well as your achievements, you will have a better chance of finding a healthy and working balance between mutuality and autonomy.

3. Understanding how emotions affect your communication patterns can lead to a reduction of day-to-day conflict. With practice you can learn to respond to what people actually say rather than what you think they may have said. Many positive statements may sound negative to you at first if your insecurities and personal prejudices get in the way. A sensitivity triggered by microscopic shifts in expression, attitude, and mood generally exists behind most expressions of anger. In fact, anger may be triggered by events completely unrelated to your relationship. By understanding your partner's sensitivities, you can bypass conflict and increase your level of genuine communication.

4. Awareness of the specific verbal and nonverbal cues that push you and your partner into nonproductive conflicts can help avert many crises. Becoming aware of this requires developing a sensitivity to minor annoyances and an ability to identify them as a source of ongoing conflict. You might, for example, try to become conscious of gestures, intonations, and "trigger words" that make you angry or defensive by listing and discussing them with your spouse. Another approach might be to record your arguments on tape, so that you can review the conflict later on, when you are both in a calmer mood, in order to determine what statements or tones precipitated defensive responses.

Recognizing and understanding your typical communicational sequences will reduce the escalation of conflict much more effectively than suppressing your frustration. Whenever you refuse to verbalize an aggravating issue, it goes underground and works its way unseen. One couple I knew experienced enormous tension over the wife's contention that the husband seemed to be "miserable" all the time. Closer examination revealed that her definition of "miserable" differed from his; only when she recognized that he was not trying to elicit guilt or sympathy when he said he had a "miserable" day could she deal with his use of the word. Realizing their different conceptions about this one "trigger word" enabled them to talk more coherently and seriously about how they actually felt about each other.

5. Focus on the positive rather than the negative as a specific technique for improving the flow of your communication—even when you are contradicting your partner or trying to force acceptance of your version of things. The importance of positive suggestion as opposed to aversive, or negative, formulations has been described by Paul Watzlawick:

> Any injunction, any instruction, is much more effective when given in positive language—that is, free from negation. "Remember to mail this letter" is bound to be remembered much more reliably . . . than "Don't forget to mail this letter. . . . The more negative and frightening a linguistic formulation, the less the other will be willing to accept it and the sooner he will forget it. Positive and concrete formulations are preconditions of any successful influence.*

People ignore attacks more than friendly, cautious approaches. In the less technical words of the proverb, you'll win over more people with honey than with vinegar.

6. In addition to *tuning in,* much can be accomplished

*Paul Watzlawick, *The Language of Change* (New York: Basic Books, 1978), pp. 67–68.

by *tuning down,* or consciously reducing the level of information two people exchange. Many people confuse high-intensity conversation with real communication, and—as we saw in the example of Paul and Vivian—the two differ. Sometimes a reduction in the sheer volume of words passed between you can work wonders. Words frequently disguise rather than illuminate meaning. An increase in the amount of silence may help you to hear what others have to say.

Ideally it makes sense to keep your opinion to yourself on certain matters, to listen rather than speak, to admit it when you don't have the answer, and to approach spontaneous outbursts of emotion (both your own and others) with caution. Having an opinion about everything—and the need to impose it on others—does not necessarily convey eagerness or willingness to communicate; it may indicate a dependent need to have others rely on you.

In the end, in order to preserve a loving relationship, you must learn to communicate on a higher level of *abstraction* than you customarily do. In fact, you must learn to communicate *about* communication, to talk about *how* you talk with each other. This literal definition of meta-communication underscores the importance of stating your own case clearly and of listening (while reserving judgment) to what your loved ones have to say.

Generally speaking, you will find it easier to express your own views than to listen to others. But people who try to do both build the most successful loving unions. In a communicational impasse, you can guarantee failure if you insist on having your own version heard first. You increase the chance for success by being willing to listen and to hear what your partner has to say.

Hearing vs. Listening

A few years back the colloquialism "I hear where you're coming from" was in fashion. "Hearing," though, is not the same thing as "listening"—as illustrated by the following anecdote.

A young man, named Jeff, wanted to visit his friend, Joan, and telephoned her to arrange the evening, fully expecting her to say "Fine."

She, however, had planned to wash her hair—nothing that might interfere with their relationship, but enough to create a fissure in their communication that night.

"I can't go out tonight," said Joan. "I really planned to stick around the house."

"That's fine with me," replied Jeff. "I'll bring over a bottle of wine."

"Well, I don't know," said Joan. "I just really want to hang around, you know? I'm not really in the mood for a party."

"Sure. Fine. I hear you. See you later, then, OK?"

"Sure. Later. OK."

And they hung up.

An hour later, to Joan's amazement, Jeff turned up at her door, ready to spend an evening at home with her—without wine, as she had demanded. He was completely shocked to discover, as she opened the door, that she hadn't wanted him around at all.

Jeff heard Joan's refusal to go out with him not as rejection but as an invitation to stay at home with her. Joan, on the other hand, thought she had made it perfectly clear, by her refusal of his bottle of wine, that she did not want company at all. Neither one tuned into the real meaning of each other's words, and though they both *heard* the actual words being spoken, neither one really *listened* to their meaning.

If Jeff had been more sensitive to the nuances of Joan's remarks, he would have sensed her reluctance to have him visit. If Joan had been more sensitive to Jeff's insistence that they spend the evening together, she would have realized that "See you later" meant in a short while. But neither one listened. Instead, they focused on what they *wanted* to hear rather than listening more carefully to the tone of the message, and this left them, ultimately, victims of an easily avoidable misunderstanding.

Hearing the spoken word presents no problems, but actually listening for the real import of the message in terms of words, tone, nuance, and the like requires more effort. Too many couples focus on the concrete words rather than the total message, and much valuable information disappears in transit, as the couples lose the opportunity to fully understand each other.

To learn to listen for the whole message requires developing the capacity to listen with what I have called the "third ear"* and to observe your behavior. You can't simply record your words, and those of your partner. You must also be able to place yourself *above* the conversation, and analyze the shape of your interactions.

You must learn, in other words, to visualize the special pattern of interaction created by you and your loved one. You must work toward the recognition that your views are only one part of a complex system that is continually being re-created by your actions and reactions to everyone else. If you can do that, you will have come a long way

*Ari Kiev, *Active Loving* (New York: Crowell, 1979), pp. 65–69.

toward resolving many of the inevitable dilemmas that plague every loving couple.

I am not suggesting that learning to listen or learning to recognize the metalanguage of your relationship will solve all your problems: some problems simply cannot be solved. But learning to relate on a metacommunicational level—learning to talk about *how* you talk together—will definitely help you determine the built-in structural dimensions of the relationship. Understanding your fixed sequencing of communications will give you a much better chance of resolving many problems.

This may not enable you to eliminate all conflict from your relationship but it should help you to discover, in a spirit of mutual cooperation, how big and unwieldy your problems typically can be—and how listening to each other can help to make them smaller.

Chapter 10

Dilemmas

"Happy families are all alike; every unhappy family is unhappy in its own way."

This is the first sentence of Tolstoi's *Anna Karenina,* and you may agree or disagree with it as you like, but it does point to the enormous range of difficulties that can characterize a troubled union. You may question if all happy marriages have some quality or qualities in common, but clearly, among the thousands of unions that end each year, no two ever dissolve for precisely the same reasons. Sexual incompatibility disrupts many relationships, while playing almost no part in others. Financial setbacks may cause breakups for some, but draw others more tightly together. The number of reasons for divorce may equal the number of reasons for marriage.

Nevertheless, relational problems can be grouped into a few general categories. The most common areas of conflict relate to sex, money, children, life style, and relationships with friends and relatives. This should not come as a surprise. In a society of rapidly changing values and living trends, you might expect frequent disagreement over child-rearing and relations with family and friends. In our rapidly shrinking economy, financial woes will have an increasing impact on people's lives. And sexuality, of course, has been a major source of interpersonal friction since Adam and Eve.

But identifying what people argue about does not really establish the root causes of their disagreements. You must make this distinction in order to understand the dilemmas of relationships. Too often, couples fighting over, say, an unbalanced bank account assume that if the husband only made more money, or the wife managed the household expenses better, their troubles would go away. This fails to take into account that the frictional *patterns* underlying most interpersonal clashes have much greater significance than the specific problems they cause.

Most of the trouble spots in close unions result from, rather than cause, dissension. This occurs frequently in sexually incompatible couples, who often seek help after experiencing problems for some time, and who generally have come to identify sex as the focus of their mutual grief. "I don't love him any more," the wife will say. "He just doesn't turn me on." Or the husband will shake his head in dismay, admitting, "We're just not happy in bed," incorrectly assuming their problem to be strictly a sexual one. I often have to explain to such couples that the failure of sex to satisfy one or both of them should be viewed not as a *coup de grâce* but as a symptom or warning sign of trouble elsewhere in the union. Sexuality—or finances, or child-rearing—may be an immediate source of friction; but it is seldom the root cause.

Various patterns of bad interaction result from different factors. While they are no easier to specify than the symptomatic issues to which they give rise, they can be generally identified, as I tried to do throughout the middle of this book, in examining how certain basic patterns of relationships consistently cause problems. In this chapter I want to review some of the basic "bad mixes" we've already mentioned, and demonstrate in greater detail how they create the recurring dilemmas of interpersonal life. Looking at the structure—the roots, if you like—of specific troubles will clarify the distinction between symptoms and causes.

Let's begin with one of the most common causes of distress: the belief, instilled in so many young people today, that marriage ought to be a way of finding "happiness."

The Search for Happiness

A popular old adage underscores the futility of making happiness a goal of romantic union. "Success," it goes, "is getting what you want. Happiness is wanting what you get."

Rather than being merely a clever inversion, this adage suggests the close link between "success" and the achievement of an external objective—that elusive "something" that lures so many to despair when they fail to achieve it. Most people make this tangible, external "success" the ultimate goal of their lives, and count themselves content, or happy, only when they have reached it. This turns the adage on its head, equating happiness and success, and making them both into external objectives to be achieved.

While success may be achieved in this way, happiness surely cannot. Quintessentially an *internal* sensation, a feeling of being at one with things as they exist, happiness by definition cannot be "captured." As Erasmus noted, "The chief point of happiness is that a man is willing to be what he is." You cannot search directly for happiness; it results indirectly from events and circumstances, reflecting an ability to flow through experiences and to accept contentment when and if it occurs.

Unfortunately, many people expect close unions to provide them with what they have not been able to find within themselves. Feeling miserable and lost in their lives, they believe that their personal problems will disappear and their feelings will be transformed into bliss if only they can find the right person. But externalizing your desires and pinning your hopes on something or someone out there—in this case a person—and expecting it to make you into something else generally does not prove successful. The unions of people who approach romance in this fashion seldom last long, for no romantic union can complete a person who feels incomplete in himself.

Of course, you may *indirectly* find happiness by trying to make someone else happy, by doing something creative, or by reaching beyond the constraints of your own self-limiting ego. If you become absorbed in your own activities and develop confidence in your own good feelings about another person without needing to look for happiness, you paradoxically have a good chance of finding it. On the other hand, if you constantly search for it, and expect your lover to give it to you as a product of your union—you will find only frustration, for you cannot accept yourself as you are, and self-acceptance is necessary to attain contentment. This means accept your "lows" as well as your "highs," and realize that no amount of effort can make your life, or anyone else's, into a rose garden. As I indicated in chapter 3, a healthy attitude consists of reducing unrealistic expectations.

Brenda, a forty-year-old divorcée, remained in an unfulfilling relationship because of a fear of loneliness. Whenever she felt pressured by her boyfriend, Will, she withdrew. This invariably led Will to criticize her, which further intensified her fear and self-doubt, and led her to accommodate him until she began to feel pressured again —and once again sought to withdraw.

Brenda was caught up in the uncertainties of the relationship. She could not tolerate the idea of being alone because she equated it with being unhappy. Treatment helped her to develop her sense of autonomy, which enabled her to tolerate her differences with Will. She became less dependent on him, found it easier to be herself, and could continue to grow in the relationship from a position of strength. Since most of her problems arose from her dependency on the relationship rather than from dissatisfaction with Will per se, their union, after she had established her independence, could begin to grow stronger.

Fundamentally, Brenda had confused her personal contentment with the smoothness of her relationship, and was not able to balance autonomy and mutuality. She and Will had created an unsatisfactory "push-pull" pattern of interacting. They both needed to learn to accept occasional conflict and develop a better sense of their own separateness so as to ride out the troubling times.

They could do this, though, only after I pointed out the regularity and predictability of the friction they generated. Like most couples, they had been locked into a rigid type of interaction—one run, in effect, by the powerful forces of inertia.

More of the Same

According to Newton's laws of motion, an object in motion remains in motion until some external influence—gravity, drag, or friction, for example—slows it down or stops it. An object at rest remains at rest until an external force—bombardment by another object, for example—sets it into motion. The same principle underlying both these situations, *inertia*, refers to the tendency for objects to remain in their current state or condition unless disturbed. This principle is as important in interpersonal relationships as in the realm of objects and forces.

We've already considered how couples fall into predictable, recurrent patterns; how a demanding spouse and a passive-aggressive spouse together can produce "a rigid-complementary" behavioral impasse; how the repetition compulsion principle operates to reproduce the neurotic patterns of childhood in adults; how individuals deny themselves by functioning in terms of typical role models of "husband" or "wife"; and how couples follow fixed roles or act out scenarios with each other, rather than improvising their own "scripts." In all of these patterns of poor interaction, the people involved adjust to difficulties by doing "more of the same" rather than by modifying their behavior. Inertia works on people in much the same way as it does on objects: most people require an external force to effect any change in their behavior.

You and your spouse form an interactional system that intricately reflects the exchange of sentiments between the two of you. Unless you become aware of this—and unless you recognize how frequently you try to deal with problems by doing more of the same things you have done before—it becomes very difficult to see your relationship realistically. It often takes a third party to objectively observe some of the unspoken rules of your relationship.

This especially holds true in the area of communications, where people commonly accept old patterns without realizing they may no longer be effective. Your relationship continually changes in response to changes in you and your spouse, yet your inertia frequently blinds you to that, allowing you to assume that your partner knows your thoughts simply because he or she has been tuned in to them well in the past.

Fred and Sylvia, for example, had not had sexual relations for four years. Sylvia could not understand Fred's fear of approaching her, since she "knew" that he "knew" that she would never reject him. I questioned her as to whether she had ever bothered to tell him that. "If you're interested," I suggested, "why not let him know it?" She was surprised and reluctant to act because she feared being seen as aggressive. But when I pointed out that she could express her interest in nonaggressive ways—by her use of perfume and attractive clothes as well as more physical expressions of tenderness—she agreed to give it a try. She soon discovered that she could signal her interest and acceptance of Fred with a warm smile and a touch of her natural coyness. Feeling more secure as a result of this behavior, Fred began to respond.

But they might not have been able to resolve this problem if an outside observer's views had not nudged them out of their self-imposed state of inertia and gotten things moving again. They had evolved a fixed system of relating that precluded change.

All unions become fixed and closed and develop unique languages for maintaining the status quo. This leads in many cases to communication blocks, which also commonly cause interpersonal strife.

Opening the Lines

By now you no doubt understand that your vocabulary, your use of language, and your basic assumptions about the world differ from your partner's. To what extent, however, do you communicate about these differences and to what extent do you mask them? The more you become aware of your habitual communication patterns, both verbal and nonverbal, the better your chance of changing ineffective, noncommunicative, or conflictual patterns. If you use your discussions and arguments to mask the issues that divide you, it is more likely that your cyclical, nonproductive bind will persist.

Remember, constraining behavior patterns will not be changed by the mere application of common sense, any more than physical habits can be modified by willpower alone. You must learn to change the underlying *rules* of your relationship in order to modify the disturbing behavior. To do this you must first recognize the *implicit fixed sequences* of reaction, and understand how you both contribute to them.

Discovering these sequences can be a difficult and unpleasant task: first, because no one enjoys discovering the predictable or fixed nature of his or her behavior; second, because looking at your particular interactions from an outside observer's viewpoint often means becoming aware of quite uncomfortable patterns in the way you relate to your spouse; and third, because changing those patterns may require that you communicate with each other, on a conscious and spoken level, things you had previously consigned to the "safer" areas of the nonverbal or the taboo.

Because of this, overcoming communication blocks often means that you must endure some uncomfortable or disquieting times. When you first begin communicating about feelings, it seems harder, not easier, because of your limited vocabulary and experience. You may even find some increase in the level of interpersonal stress. This is disturbing, to be sure, but the short-term stress of open communication almost always produces less damage than the long-range stress that follows conciliation.

As we have seen throughout this book, to improve interpersonal communication you must learn how to deal with unpleasant emotions as well as pleasant ones. In any union you have to strive for the development of enough interpersonal *trust* to allow you to speak freely, without fearing that you will injure your partner or that he or she will injure you. In good relationships, people accept each other enough to be able to tolerate each other's quirks—to accept each other warts and all.

This can prove difficult to achieve, because interpersonal trust cannot be developed merely by agreement, and it can be blocked by automatic responses to nonverbal cues or trigger words. To develop mutual trust you must be genuine and spontaneous, and run the risk of triggering conflictual responses. Here again, cooperation provides the key to perceiving and transmuting friction.

Everyone fails sometime. Everyone reneges on obligations and promises, or acts insensitively to another's needs. At such times you had best hope your partner is strong enough and trusts you enough to forgive you. When you come to recognize how unsatisfactory your behavior has been, you should talk with your spouse about it and try to come to terms on how to prevent future recurrences. Recrimination and fault-finding will affect both of you equally, while talking calmly about events will serve to open the lines and put your conflict in a new light.

This doesn't necessitate "full disclosure" about everything you think and do. Such openness doesn't ensure success. Indeed, just the opposite may result. While openness about your feelings can be valuable, you need not wear your heart on your sleeve, nor should you feel guilty if you keep some things to yourself as a way of maintaining autonomy or preserving your relationship. Don't confuse keeping a secret with telling a lie. In fact, the need to know things that are kept secret often reflects a transferred dependency, which may interfere with the natural flow of communication.

My experience in counseling Joanne, a young editor whose husband, Steve, insisted on her telling him in detail everything about her life, illustrates the dilemmas raised by an excessive commitment to "honesty."

"He says he wants to know all about me," she complained. "He doesn't care what I do, as long as I let him know. Do I have to tell him?"

"If you want honesty," I explained to her, "you have to be willing to let communication flow spontaneously—even to the point of not getting all the answers. Steve wants to monitor your thoughts and your activity. If you comply with this, you'll be functioning like a robot."

"But don't I owe him that much?" she protested. "Isn't it his right to know?"

"It's your right to decide what you want to talk about. You have to decide whether you want to compromise your integrity for the sake of the relationship. It seems to me that being *who you want to be* has greater priority than the obligation to reveal yourself to anyone. Ideally you ought to be able to see what the two of you are doing and establish a mutually agreed upon set of rules."

"But he can't handle that. He's got to know who I'm with, why, where . . . everything. It's starting to drive me crazy."

"Whose problem is it, then? His or yours?"

It was, of course, a mutual problem—a dilemma created by Steve's demand for a full accounting and by Joanne's uncertainty about whether to go along with his demands. She had to differentiate between choosing to communicate and an exploitative demand for information that too often is confused with "honesty." In many cases, "telling all" can be harmful to others and create more tensions than before.

If you want your relationship to prosper, you have no moral obligation to give your mate constant and straightforward accounts of how you feel about things. Sometimes silence can avoid confrontation. Imagine how thorny a relationship would be if a husband felt morally obliged to criticize his wife's hairdo or if the wife felt obliged to tell her husband every time someone whistled at her on the street. A constant, in-depth review of such issues really only serves to overload the lines between two people until they finally short out.

A complex variation of this can seen in the case of affairs.

Affairs: The Major Threat

Several recent popular books and surveys on American sexual mores suggested that one out of two married men and women have extramarital sexual relations at some point in the course of their marriage.* These figures reflect a shift from puritanical traditions or an expression of strain in modern relationships, depending on your viewpoint. Whatever the explanation, no one doubts that an affair can evoke jealousy, competitiveness, fear, and a whole range of emotions that can destroy a relationship. Most couples lack the skills to handle adequately the volatile emotions provoked by the discovery of infidelity. Even the *suspicion* of it can create havoc, since more often than not it's the response to the discovery rather than the affair itself that sets a crisis in motion.

An affair can produce a real dilemma by reducing the incentive to resolve marital differences. Indeed, the reassurance and support received from an affair may reduce the motivation to continue in the marriage—especially since affairs so often stimulate unrealistic expectations about eventual happiness with the new, "right" partner.

Affairs require considerable energy and motivation and involve much time and thought. Uncluttered by the mundane pressures of daily living, they have many intense elements of excitement and short-term gratification built into them, which give them an illusory dimension of validity and meaningfulness and can make a long-term relationship seem banal by comparison.

But affairs generate severe anxieties, especially a heightened sense of separation, uncertainty, and exploitation. That's why the discovery of an extramarital affair can fracture the sense of trust, and complicate the chances of resolving a shaky marriage.

How can a loving couple deal with this sensitive issue? First, consider my comments about full disclosure. In

*See Mary Bartusis, *Every Other Man* (New York: Dutton, 1978), and Lewis Yablonsky, *The Extra-Sex Factor* (New York: Times Books, 1978).

general, confessing to an affair in the spirit of openness can be counterproductive, since the resulting confrontations may impede further communication. Most such confessions reflect a search for approval rather than an effort at honesty. At times a confession may even be a manipulative effort to elicit punishment, which thereby absolves the guilt. In fact, ending an affair and living with your guilt may prove the least disruptive way to deal with it.

Ending an affair may not be easy, since it may mean giving up the psychological satisfaction that it has been providing, and also because affairs provide an excuse for not accepting responsibility for yourself. This holds true not only for the person having the affair but also for the cuckolded spouse who may tolerate an affair because of the fear of a blowup, or because it provides a reason to hold on to anger, however repressed. Tolerance of painful experiences keeps your own feelings out of awareness and mistakenly reinforces the assumption that to let go of your feelings would expose you to conflict and pain.

Even if you decide to bring things out into the open, the resolution of extramarital affairs can be complicated because of the difficulty of expressing your feelings clearly and simply, without fear of consequences. Revealing your hurt feelings without threats or controlling behavior may help to overcome an impasse. Even if you inform your spouse of your distress about the affair, you can avoid dictating how he or she should behave, so as to leave room to decide what he or she wants to do. By focusing only on your own feelings, and not on how "bad" the sinner is, you may make it easier for your partner to talk about what led him or her to become involved in the affair in the first place.

An affair generally results from various types of inadequacy and discontent in the relationship. Recognizing it as the result of some interactive process, rather than simply as a unilateral expression of disinterest, puts you in a better position to find the factors missing in your relationship, or to develop better skills at negotiating and resolving conflict. An affair need not lead to the end of your marriage. According to Israel Charney, an affair provides:

> a test of the capacity of both spouses to bear an awareness of their real separateness from one another; and a test of their capacity to bear an awareness of the hatred of one another; and a test of their capacity to bear an awareness of the evil potential of one another; and with all this, to affirm a wish to be in union.*

An affair, therefore, can bring a couple together in the recognition of their mutual frailty and their mutual willingness to accept conflict and change as an essential part of any long-term union.

Other Sexual Dilemmas

While affairs reflect the inability of couples to manage sexuality in a smooth and uncomplicated manner, they make up only the tip of the sexual iceberg. Countless other behavior patterns reflect cultural rigidities about sexuality.

Consider the idealized myth of correct male and female social roles. Timid, demure, and virginal, the ideal woman awaits a knight on a white horse. Dominant, aggressive, competent, the mythical male seeks a virgin to protect, then deflower, then abandon. To the extent that this

*Israel Charney, *Marital Love and Hate* (New York: Macmillan, 1972), p. 135.

mythical ideal influences the romantic behavior of young couples, it creates many sexual problems.

As long as a man and a woman remain just "friends," they have access to a relatively easily managed range of interpersonal behavior. Once they become lovers, their options narrow and they become prey to many misconceptions, conventional social roles, and interactional *prescriptions*, which encourage passive acceptance and emotional confusion. This can be quite problematic and contradictory to the norms associated with friendship patterns.

Knowing a variety of dating and courting patterns does not constitute the real challenge in developing a relationship, at least in the early, or approach, phase. Letting *friendship* evolve first, and then transforming it, without pressure, into romance constitutes the real challenge. It is a challenge that few people meet, since the acceptance of friendship before sex runs counter to many approved norms of behavior. As conventional dictum goes, "bed first, talk later."

In line with the mass media emphasis on the adolescent playboy fantasy, some people believe that a productive union can follow only from sexual "conquest and surrender." Since just the opposite usually occurs, many current relationships experience a great strain because of the discrepancy between the fantasy and the reality. Such fantasies almost preclude the chance of developing a genuine friendship with your prospective spouse before sharing the physical manifestation of romance.

Carol demonstrated the kind of problems that can result from involvement in a sexual relationship before a friendship has developed. She visited my office for help in dealing with the problem of maintaining a heavy social schedule and preserving her virginity. Convinced that her self-image required both, she found herself in a perpetual bind. "I'm getting so pressured to get into bed," she said, "I just can't think straight. The men today won't let up. Last Friday night, back in my apartment, my date really started to hassle me."

"In your apartment?" I asked. "A bad place to go, wasn't it?"

"Yes, it's a bad place to go," she admitted, "but what do you do after you've had dinner? There's no place to go, nothing else to do. We went to a disco later, but when you get back from that you have the same problem again."

"Why can't you just simply say, 'Thanks, I've had a pleasant evening, good night'?"

"I'm afraid if I do that, no one will call me again."

"So you invite your dates in," I said, "thinking that if you don't, you'll hurt their feelings. But they don't know that. They interpret your invitation differently. They hear what they want to hear, and maybe also something that you've been communicating nonverbally."

"But I don't want them to feel totally rejected," she said.

"For whose sake?" I replied. "Yours or theirs? You've got to make the decisions for your own life. What you're doing now is playing the coy, come-hither role, and letting them play the wolves. Naturally it's not working out. It can work out only when you realize you don't owe anyone an explanation or an apology for not going to bed with them. When you realize that, then you will be able to say no to those you want to say no to, and you will say yes only to the person you do want to go to bed with."

Ultimately, Carol began to see that she had been setting herself up for rejection by giving her dates mixed signals.

This frustrated them and intensified her sense of guilt. She had to learn to relate to men not in the "expected" manner, but as she wanted to relate at that time. That, I assured her, would make her no less attractive—and might eliminate the men who insisted on getting their own way.

Carol's case illustrates a common dilemma in modern relationships characterized by the man's "need" to prove his masculinity by sexual "performance" and the woman's "need" to appear receptive. The dilemma reflects the mistake of allowing others—be they friends, lovers, or newspaper columnists—to dictate how the relationship should evolve. Rather than rely on their own intuition, many people surrender to the dictates of society, and remain pawns in their own games.

Developing a good relationship means evolving your *own* definition of what you want and need irrespective of prevailing social conventions. It means, in short, becoming your own person.

Your Own Person

"Something there is that doesn't love a wall," wrote Robert Frost. People in relationships often try to abolish all of the "walls" between them in order to achieve unity. In doing so, they often destroy their own integrity, which should nourish the growth of the relationship. Forgetting that "good fences make good neighbors," they chip away at the barriers, and succeed only in tearing each other and their relationship apart.

This leads to one of the most serious and common dilemmas of close unions, reflecting the inability to develop a balance between mutuality and autonomy. In their zeal to guarantee mutual growth, lovers often kill the uniqueness and spontaneity of those they love by insisting on togetherness rather than tolerating autonomy.

To avoid this problem, you have to recognize that however close your union with another person, each of you has a separateness that must be protected. Most people recognize this, and yet they respond to it by rushing dependently into the arms of partners who allow them to forget it. I have seen literally hundreds of close unions built on a mutual denial of human aloneness—and only a handful or so built on an awareness of the fact.

Appreciating and exploring your separateness can actually help you overcome loneliness, while trying to convince yourselves that you're two peas in a pod will only frustrate you and damage your interaction. Accepting your own uniqueness and periodic sense of isolation from each other, recognizing your fragility, and recognizing that you can't always be synchronized with each other, will in the long run help you achieve a firmer union.

Formal rituals solidify relationships and convince people that their initial, intense feelings of togetherness will always remain as keen as they were at the beginning. But if you believe the social myth of "togetherness forever," you surrender yourself to an artifice: thinking that you have no problems and have tuned into each other actually demonstrates one of love's most difficult dilemmas—the need to eliminate through union your sense of aloneness. People who appreciate their "fences," on the other hand —considering them as existential symbols or as things to lean on and chat—have a better chance at both personal and interpersonal health.

Real togetherness, in other words, stems from acknowledging your aloneness. To accomplish this may require that you experience a thousand cycles of coming together and moving apart; it may require that you live together for fifty years. It takes time to accept the uncertainty of love but you will be better off if you recognize the insecurity of life than if you continue to try to make it go away. Holding on to the "togetherness" façade can be a problem for everyone, since real openness, real togetherness, differs both from the popular image of it and from the image of togetherness you may project to the world.

Generally people share only public images; but they need to learn to share the hollowness, the small voices of fear and loneliness and anger that the images conceal. You can do that only by accepting and communicating your fundamental vulnerability—your aloneness in the midst of closeness—a paradox so awesome, in fact, that you will want to share it with someone you love.

The paradoxical effect of aloneness enriching a twosome frequently can be seen among couples temporarily separated testing out new ways of relating to each other. Most people view separation as proof of the relationship's failure, when it really can reflect regeneration. During separation you have an opportunity to reassume personal responsibility, rediscover inner strengths and internal rhythms, and establish new interests. This can be an opportunity to grow, for learning to contend with freedom and loneliness helps you to develop a fuller and more intense relationship.

This is not necessarily the case. A separation may be the prelude to a breakup, or it may be a healthy force for change. Whether it enriches or destroys your relationship depends on the strength of your relationship when you separate. A separation affords you an opportunity to regain your sense of uniqueness and autonomy; with luck, when you reunite they will breathe new life into your relationship. If, however, you reactivate the old dependent pattern of relating, you may experience false expectations, circular binds, and disappointments once again.

The ideal would be to develop this exciting sense of uniqueness *while you are together*. The people involved in good, working close relationships tend their fences lovingly, and don't need to maintain constant control or even contact to convince each other of their love. Confident individuals see their partners' love as a gift, not as a need, and they recognize the instability and uncertainty of life, in which nothing remains as it was, but is in continual flux.

In the strongest unions, then, uncertainty is seen as a plus, because it keeps alive the separateness so crucial for realizing a genuine togetherness.

Chapter 11

Conclusion: Harnessing Conflict

In his dialogue *Phaedrus,* Plato compared the soul, or psyche, of human beings to a charioteer controlling a team of spirited and incompatible horses. A good "driver" would be emotionally and mentally capable of controlling his inner thoughts and passions; a bad driver would let these thoughts and passions take over, until they ran him off the road.

The same metaphor applies to the emotional life of loving couples. Even when two people genuinely commit themselves to a relationship, a certain amount of friction between them inevitably appears. Like the charioteer's horses, people have unique temperaments, and no linking of two or more people can occur without friction. Since dissension inevitably occurs, you need to learn how to control your own passions, so that trouble, when it occurs, doesn't drive you off the road.

This doesn't mean dissension is a "bad" thing. Actually, it may be a healthy sign of vital involvement, an indication of the fact that the two of you are exchanging energy back and forth. "The worst sin towards our fellow creatures," said Bernard Shaw, "is not to hate them, but to be indifferent to them." The presence of conflict indicates an abiding interpersonal interest.

Conflict rarely produces beneficial results, however. Most interpersonal tension reflects bitter, repetitive, and counterproductive sentiments whose causes and circular nature have not been grasped by the people involved. In many relationships, a counterproductive interaction pattern aggravates tension and rides the couple to despair. There's a difference between healthy and unhealthy conflict, and to make conflict *productive,* you must harness your interpersonal tensions so that they enrich rather than diminish your life.

Achieving this kind of control over conflict involves four basic steps.

First, you must recognize that a problem exists, and appreciate it as a reflection of good energy rather than as a sign of failure. At the same time, you must examine the *sources* of your conflict, and review your unresolved problems from the past, including those relating to dependency, jealousy, self-image, and the constantly shifting equilibrium between mutuality and autonomy.

Second, you must accept your share of the responsibility for the creation of your difficulties—and for finding their solutions.

Third, you must *believe* you can change; you must overcome the fear that this is impossible.

Finally, you must develop basic *communication* and *negotiation* skills for handling and minimizing conflict; you must make a shared commitment to use these skills in harnessing your conflict.

Each of these four steps of conflict management may be viewed as if they were points on an equestrian course.

The first three relatively small steps might be compared to hurdles. The last step—the acquisition of conflict management skills—requires more experience and skill and may be viewed as a much higher hurdle, or a wall.

Hurdle 1: Denial

Denial by one or both parties that a problem exists at all accounts for a large portion of the difficulties encountered by couples in conflict. The refusal to acknowledge a problem makes it extremely difficult to recognize the need for conflict management.

I've described the "terrible simplifications" that loving couples often impose on each other in lieu of recognizing their tensions. Such simplifications can impede communication, since seeing things through rose-colored glasses only leads to greater confusion and resentment in the end. The tendency to ignore or shun conflict can be a major problem. Often, sensing a brewing conflict, people go overboard trying to deny its importance. Or, conversely, they recognize the tension but deal with it by arguing all the more loudly. Both approaches increase incompatibility.

In cases of ongoing or developing tension, two people must be willing to acknowledge the problem as something more than a combination of their criticisms of each other. They must see that any interpersonal problem takes *work* to be solved. Many couples fall apart at this point. While acknowledging the tension, they refuse to recognize the need for a new type of communication. Instead they hope that time or natural processes will solve their problems—and they end up only with "more of the same."

The first principle of enhanced communication is the *acceptance of the need* for it, and the simultaneous agreement that emotional outbursts have no place in harnessing tension. A couple with real affection for each other must agree to cooperate to control momentary passions until they can work toward resolution.

Acknowledging the existence of the problem, though, must be followed by some inquiry into its causes and the factors that have kept it going. A couple striving to pass this first hurdle must be willing to review their individual and collective histories to find which legacies of the past are merely being rerun in the present.

I am not suggesting an absorption in the past to the exclusion of the present, only a periodic review of the past that might help in the anticipation of possible errors in judgment, and in the selection of alternatives that will increase future options. Clearing the first hurdle involves a commitment to changing your habits, dependency binds, and even the rules of your relationship. Understanding the evolution of your problems will help you to do this intelligently and dispassionately.

Hurdle 2: Blame

The problems you and your spouse experience as parts of an interactional system cannot be attributed to either of you alone: understanding the structure of your relationship ought to help you to see how both of you contribute to the problems you experience.

Unfortunately, most people do not choose this rational approach. Blaming others can be more comfortable than blaming yourself. You may be guilty of attributing responsibility for the problem and its correction to your partner, having accepted the illusion of unilateral fault. This kind of shifting of blame, of denying complicity in the tensions of a bad interaction, constitutes the second major hurdle to interpersonal growth.

This occurs often. I have seen countless couples who, even after acknowledging that they understood how they created problems together, continued to assign the solution to their partner. Recognizing the commonly occurring dilemma created by a combination of male silence and wifely nagging, the wife may still insist that "Roger has got to talk more," while he may insist, with equal conviction, that "Hilary's got to get off my back." Identifying the source of the problem as outside of themselves, neither of them changes anything.

Demanding that your partner initiate constructive change minimizes your responsibility and assures you that everything will remain the same. Expecting someone to do something *because you say so* creates a psychological impasse or paradoxical inhibition. By making a demand, you often make it impossible for your spouse to do what you ask.

If you really want to make conflict productive, you must concentrate only on changing *yourself,* and learn to control the natural inclination to impose solutions on your spouse. Only by changing yourself can you induce real change in another person.

In order to change, you must learn to observe yourself so as to become more aware of your automatic behavior patterns. Consider how you typically respond and behave in certain situations. Do you become sullen or cooperative when someone asks you to do something? Do you use sarcasm or other put-downs unconsciously? What nonverbal cues do you transmit to others? Do you listen, or only hear? Becoming aware of your typical patterns will in time give you more opportunity to change them, and to *choose* to act in the way you want to act. This will be the key to your future development.

To bring about a change in any interactional system, both parties must change. Since you cannot force change in another person, you must therefore focus on your *own* behavior as the essential lever of enhanced communication and cooperation.

Hurdle 3: Fear

Those of you old enough to remember Mickey Mantle, the home-run king of the Yankees, may also remember Jim Piersall, a contemporary of his. Piersall, an accomplished ballplayer, experienced a nervous breakdown during the late 1950s because he was terrified of what he perceived as his declining ability. Once a strong player, he found his performance slipping until, just before his collapse, he seemed unable to play at all.

Eventually, Piersall recovered and wrote a book about his experience, *Fear Strikes Out,* which underscored with poignant precision how uncertainty over success can become a self-fulfilling prophecy, ensuring the very failure that has been feared. Fear of failure not only nearly ruined Piersall's career, but has been, and continues to be, a major obstacle to productive communication in good relationships.

While you may recognize your problems and commit yourself to change, you may be inclined to make only a halfhearted commitment, and in the end this will keep you from clearing the third hurdle. Like the horse who may be undone by hesitation at the jump, you may find yourself unable to move out of your old, recurrent patterns, simply because you believe you cannot change.

Most people steer clear of committing themselves entirely to a goal, especially one as touchy and complicated as interpersonal change. Comfortable with the familiar, they give less than 100 percent of their energies to the project, and then wonder why they don't succeed. Inside they still half believe that, as Samuel Beckett put it, "There is nothing to be done." So they end up locked into old roles, old patterns, familiar unpleasantness, rather than make the leap into the unknown.

Various psychological experiments have shown that fruitful change requires a positive frame of mind. One of the most interesting experiments suggests that an optimistic "world image" may be an essential aspect of self-preservation itself. In this study, experimenters placed rats in tanks of water to measure the connection between effort and belief in success. Watzlawick reported on the findings:

> It would appear that rats that fall into water will die long before reaching the state of final physical exhaustion if by swimming around they have "convinced" themselves that there is no way of saving themselves by climbing out. But if such a rat is picked out of the water in time, this rescue leads to a decisive change in its "world image." Instead of giving up and drowning upon realization of the hopelessness of the situation, it will, when the experiment is repeated, continue to swim until total exhaustion.*

In effect, hope, or the expectation of success, can impel rats to extraordinary effort, while despair, or the expecta-

*Paul Watzlawick, *The Language of Change* (New York: Basic Books: 1978), pp. 43–44.

tion of failure, leads them to surrender to the inevitable long before they have spent all their physical energy. These findings have profound implications for human beings, and particular relevance to the kind of effort needed to transform conflict into enrichment. Fear of striking out generally leads to striking out, while the conviction that you can improve your relationship will actually help you to make it better.

You can learn to be optimistic and to cultivate an expectation of success. With effort you will begin to discover an enormous power within yourself and within your relationship. You can overcome the fear of failure by realizing that your recurrent conflicts constitute a failure in themselves, and by recognizing that *chancing* failure provides the only way out of your present dilemma.

Learning to Negotiate

Having successfully overcome these three hurdles, you are still confronted with the problem of how to negotiate. With the best of intentions, a couple may still reach an impasse if they have not learned the specific negotiation skills for defusing conflict and transforming tension into positive energy. If they fail to see how "hot topics" result from rather than cause dissension, they may become defensive and hostile rather than seek to negotiate. This can only intensify their problems.

Learning how to argue is the lesson of the rest of this chapter. What I'll give you here is certain techniques of effective arguing that will keep you from dissipating your energy in circular recriminations.

1. *Delaying your reactions.* For the twenty-sixth time this month, your spouse has left the cap off the toothpaste.

You're about to boil. What do you do? Blow up, or wait to calm down? While a quick burst of anger might seem to prevent the buildup of frustration, it seldom serves the purpose of effective communication. Many arguments can be avoided if the parties involved simply agree to *delay their responses* before attacking each other.

Delaying your reactions in a heated situation allows you to reflect momentarily on your responsibility for your present difficulties, and to reduce the impact of emotionality on your behavior. In a state of panic, emotionality may constrict your thinking, reduce the breadth of your memory span, and lead you to make decisions on the basis of insufficient information and distorted thinking. Waiting can help you avoid this.

Unfortunately, postponement may be difficult to achieve, since in an argument you may screen out the advance cues of escalating conflict so effectively that you become fully embroiled in an antagonistic discussion before you realize it.

That's why it's important to tune in to *developing* tension. Once you can recognize the beginning of an argument, you can learn to delay your reactions. Rather than arguing a point, practice standing outside the argument for a moment so as to review the events and words that may have led up to it. By avoiding prompt attack, you will reduce defensiveness and increase the chance of searching together for a negotiated solution.

2. *Using "playback."* Once you've stopped and quieted down, you'll hear more clearly what you and your partner have been saying, and hopefully will also listen to the subtle messages being transmitted. A useful technique for doing this is to visualize your mind as a continuously running tape machine, which records your words as well as

your unexpressed thoughts and nonverbal cues. Imagine that this invisible mental tape stores all the information passing between you and your spouse. By reviewing the tapes on this recorder from time to time, you can tune into levels of conversation that might originally have escaped you, and in that way obtain an overall, more objective view of the typical quality of your exchanges.

So much information passes between two people in an argument that the messages being transmitted can easily be lost if you concentrate too much on particular points. Couples sometimes argue about embarassing public behavior. In the heat of an ensuing argument the message "You hurt my feelings by ignoring me" may be drowned out by particular complaints ("You got me the wrong drink") or actual evasions ("I didn't want to go in the first place"). Playback of such a disturbing scene will enable you to review what went wrong and why, and give you useful data on the patterns that led up to the outburst.

Reviewing events together can improve communication. Unfortunately, most couples withdraw from each other when they feel hurt or misunderstood rather than express their true feelings of anger or fear. They forget that withdrawal only intensifies resentment, and that only by expressing feelings and reviewing the memory tape again can interaction improve and mutual attack be avoided.

Some couples find it useful to keep actual written or audio-tape records of their conflicts, so as to be able to compare notes after a fight. If they have tape-recorded a disagreement, they have a clear, unbiased account of the event, which they can review and discuss afterward. Effective negotiation can begin, after all, only when two people have an objective notion of the reasons for fighting. Note pads and tape recorders help to provide some objectivity. In the privacy of your own home, a tape recorder can be very helpful, as an electronic "third eye," helping both of you to see patterns that might ordinarily go unnoticed.

3. *Reframing your experiences.* Custom plays an insidious and tenacious role in human interaction. Various manifestations of inertia—repetition compulsions, role-playing, systemic interaction, dependency binds—help to maintain the status quo in relationships. One way of changing the status quo and escaping interactional impasses is to alter or *reframe* your perspective, which allows you to see your mutual rancor in a different light.

Reframing can produce change without changing the basic situation. A conscious effort to ask a spouse to relax, or to have an orgasm, or to be spontaneous, may produce the opposite effect, since once you ask someone to do something, he or she cannot respond spontaneously to any request. I have observed this in many couples with sexual problems. The more Sheila's husband, Roy, pressed her to relax and have an orgasm, the more she resisted, became self-conscious about her "inadequacies," and moved even further away from sexual fulfillment. By discussing their fears and doubts about their own sexuality in treatment, they redefined the problem, began to overcome their mutual shyness, and improved their sexual life.

Focusing on the solutions to problems rather than the problems themselves, in other words, can eliminate much of the difficulty created by efforts to solve problems. Since the solutions sometimes create more confusion and conflict than the original problems, reframing makes sense.

Changing your concept of a problem changes its meaning, thereby altering its effects.

4. *Scheduling your fights.* Conflict inevitably occurs. No matter how loving your relationship, you can't escape interpersonal tension entirely.

An effective negotiating technique for harnessing this tension requires that a couple *plan* their fights ahead of time, setting aside a given time and place each week to air grievances and review their typical responses to each other. Such "timed focus sessions" have great value in helping couples in therapy to reframe, and thus defuse, aggression.

If you have sporadic and damaging conflicts, scheduled fights will enable you to control consciously what you now do impulsively. If you schedule your fights, spontaneous uncontrolled aggression will be less likely to erupt. You will gain new insights into how you behave under stress by stepping outside the situation. This will reinforce the possibilities for change, since you and your partner will now be able to actively evaluate a response that had been negative and automatic.

Mel and Jean battled constantly for thirty-five years and sought help only when they could no longer tolerate the anguish. I suggested that they schedule their fights to gain control over them. They expressed much doubt.

"But I don't like to fight," protested Mel.

"You end up fighting anyway," I replied, "as if compelled unconsciously to fight. By doing it consciously according to mutually agreed upon rules, you'll be in a better position to change your automatic behavior."

"What do you mean about 'rules'?" asked Jean.

"No matter how you're feeling, each day set a specific half-hour aside to argue about something."

"Have an argument?" They both looked skeptical. "Even if there's nothing we feel we want to argue about?"

"You have a thirty-five-year list of topics," I said.

"What if we're not feeling hostility at that moment?" asked Jean.

She had touched on the key to their problem. They wanted to fight only when they felt angry—when they could be *absolved of the responsibility for their behavior.* What they had to learn to do was to express their feelings at other times, not simply when they felt angry. In that way, they would "make the covert overt," and take responsibility for their feelings. With practice, they did learn to fight on a regular schedule, and it greatly enhanced their ability to communicate.

The root issue is communication. Learning to negotiate and learning to express feelings, as in scheduled fighting, can harness conflict and enhance communication, and this will keep your relationship alive.

5. *Redefining yourselves.* Several times in this book I've suggested that romantic liaisons are often based on illusions rather than reality. Young people, influenced by popular romantic myths, expect relationships to solve problems, save emotional lives, and transform dreams into fact. When this doesn't happen—when they discover the confusion and fallibility of their partners—conflict erupts, the union undergoes unexpected changes, and many matches break up.

This pattern would be modified if more couples periodically looked closely at themselves and their objectives, periodically reassessed their interactions, worked for better negotiations, and together designed plans for improvement. All relationships continually evolve, but in the best relationships flux becomes a spur to mutual self-actualization. "The life which is unexamined," said Socrates, "is not worth living." The same might be said about relationships.

In most relationships, decisions about conflict and change result not from rational processes but from limited information, filtered through each person's self-image, self-esteem, and desire to avert negative feelings of guilt or anxiety. Couples in conflict seldom use decision-making procedures effectively; they fail to search for ways to reduce friction, and they rarely ask, "How can we change our lives so that both of us are satisfied?" Instead, they act *automatically* and *defensively* to justify their individual objectives, which intensifies rather than minimizes conflict. Ultimately, in this kind of situation, anxiety replaces openness, and a heightened dependency restrains individual and collective freedom.

Few couples can sensibly and calmly define the real objectives and goals of their unions. Beginning from the false expectations of the courtship period, they fail to ask each other, or themselves, what they can realistically expect from mutuality, and so they do not investigate how their mutuality fails to live up to its potential. If you don't know what you want from your union, after all, you severely limit what you will be able to get out of it.

For this reason, I advise my patients periodically to discuss with each other the unwritten rules of the relationship. Too many couples decide to live together with the assumption that they can always say "the hell with it" and run if things don't work out. A firmer commitment to togetherness, which incorporates the inevitability of tension, is what builds successful relationships.

Redefining your union must proceed from this acceptance of conflict. Techniques of negotiating and improving communication will not help you if you believe that conflict must be avoided at all costs. Such an attitude will only ensure resentment and failure. A healthy union should allow you to accept the differences that divide you, and make them work on your behalf.

Making It Work for You

In the introduction to this book, I suggested that the progress of a loving union might be likened to the erratic, uncertain journey of a boat down a wild, white water river. I presented evidence of the inevitability and usefulness of the "white water," or turbulent and everchanging motion of human interactions. The failure to acknowledge the turbulence can weaken rather than strengthen a relationship. In fact, a good relationship requires attention to the swirling, difficult uncertainty of mutual growth: the understanding that rapids play an integral role in the "river" of life, and that success in interpersonal communication means taking advantage of them.

Take advantage of the "rough" spots. Viewing the rapids as something to avoid will only cause you to end up, like Jack's nervous friend in the introduction, about to fall in the water. Seeing the "rapids" as an opportunity for growth, for testing yourself and your partner against the many daily difficulties of life together, will ensure that you will be able to assimilate conflict and change, and use them to make your union grow.

The wild and raging currents of interpersonal communication often create a desire to retreat, to minimize psychological anguish. Considering the pain that close union often causes, you can understand why many would-be lovers end up cynical and bitter early in life, convinced that "true love" can hold nothing for them but hardship and disappointment.

But this is usually their own fault. If you enter the river expecting a placid ride, you *will* be disappointed. If you enter with trepidation, assuming that the waters will be rough, you will have a better chance of avoiding the rocks and of riding the rapids to a calm, if temporary, haven. "Forewarned is forearmed." Relationships that view conflict as an ineradicable part of life, rather than an unnameable demon, stand the best chance of surviving the squalls and close calls of daily life.

The hopeful but wary lover can look at "white water" in two ways. You can imagine it as "bad" and avoidable: something which, with the right tone of voice and the right tilt of your head, you need never deal with at all. Or, you can see it as an inescapable and potentially useful source of energy, with the power to enrich and revitalize your union. This is the way an engineer sees a river—as something that, properly dammed up, can be of benefit. From a psychological viewpoint, this is a sensible approach: accepting and using conflicts can be far more productive than pretending that they will eventually disappear. The energy that passes between two people in a close union can be "tapped" just as white water can be turned into light.

Conflict and change can be a major stimulus to true growth, a source of energy that will not only keep your love alive but will nourish it in uncertain hope, so that day by day, in numerous small ways, you can become the vital, independent, and loving couple that you have it in you to be.